Collecting Cast Iron

7 55

1

Collecting
Cast Iron

Alex Ames

Moorland Publishing

📖 British Library Cataloguing in Publication Data

Ames, A
    Collecting cast iron.
    1. Ironwork - Collectors and collecting
    2. Cast-iron
    I. Title
    739'.4   NK8204

    ISBN 0-86190-001-4

739.4
A

ISBN 0 86190 001 4

Typeset by Alacrity Phototypesetters,
Banwell Castle, Weston-super-Mare, Avon
and printed in Great Britain by
Redwood Burn Ltd, Trowbridge and Esher for
Moorland Publishing Co Ltd,
9-11 Station Street, Ashbourne, Derbyshire, DE6 1DZ, England

Contents

Preface / 6
1 Introducing Cast Iron / 7
2 Cast Iron in Architecture / 15
3 Cooking and Keeping Warm / 23
4 Clean, Neat and Wholesome / 40
5 At the Door and About the House / 60
6 Miniature Grates and Mantel Ornaments / 84
7 Iron for Everything / 95
8 Collecting, Cleaning and Display / 130
Museums Displaying Cast Iron / 135
Bibliography / 136
Acknowledgements / 139
Index /141

Preface

This is a book for collectors. It is also for anyone interested in articles made from iron during the 200 years which commenced when Abraham Darby first successfully used coke for smelting iron in about 1709. Its aim is to stimulate greater interest in looking for and collecting objects of cast iron whether they be beautiful or utilitarian, and by so doing encourage their preservation. Even more important, it is hoped that museums, many of whose storehouses are filled with relics of the 'pre-plastic' age, will find space and time to mount displays so that the public can see what they have. These cannot fail to have immediate impact, revealing as they will the origins of our present way of life.

Because photographs quickly supply a near maximum information, making words partly redundant, the content is largely pictorial and as far as possible the real thing has been painstakingly searched out and photographed; but where rarity or time, or both have put the authentic article out of the author's reach then copies of pages from old catalogues have been used as illustrations. As a side effect the use of old catalogues will, perhaps, make salvage of these valuable sources of information a much more urgent matter. No attempt has been made to describe the technology of iron founding. There is already a copious literature on the subject to which the interested reader is referred.

1 Introducing Cast Iron

The art of iron founding is far from new. By the end of the second century AD the Chinese knew how to melt iron, pour it into moulds and make tools, vessels, small pieces of sculpture and cannon. In Europe, on the other hand, cast iron was not in common use until the fifteenth century. Early English founders, like the Chinese, made pots and cannon and in addition they manufactured firebacks, grave slabs and fire dogs, and the industry was heavily concentrated in the Kent and Sussex Weald. Here two most important raw materials were readily available — iron ore and wood for the charcoal used as fuel in the smelting process. This method of purifying iron was, however, terribly wasteful of wood since one acre of forest was required to give, at the most, twelve tons of charcoal, which in turn would produce less than seven tons of pig iron.

By the middle of the sixteenth century so many forests had disappeared at so fast a rate for glass making, iron founding and ship building that the Government of Queen Elizabeth I took a hand. Laws were passed making it illegal to make charcoal for iron-founding except in Kent and these laws caused foundrymen to move into more remote areas where wood burning was not prohibited. They also set men to searching for other fuels with which to melt their ore: coal being the most obvious. The first attempts using raw coal were doomed to failure although Dud Dudley, illegitimate son of Lord Derby, received much publicity from his claim to have succeeded. Only when Abraham Darby moved from Bristol, where he had been working, to Coalbrookdale in Shropshire, in order to revive an already existing foundry, was the secret found.

In Bristol, it appears, Darby had used, or knew of the use of, coke — coal burned in a restricted supply of oxygen — as a fuel, and this knowledge directed his first experiments and in turn led to its use in the foundry. The story of his triumph in 1709 has already been told in detail by others and need not be repeated here, although anyone interested would be advised to read at least one of Arthur Raistrick's books mentioned in the bibliography. There were technical problems with the first coke-smelted cast iron. They, and prejudice, delayed replacement of charcoal iron for years, but by the last quarter of the eighteenth century the new method had made much progress and to a large extent had replaced the old method. Emphasis of some of the advantages of cast iron — it is strong under heavy compression loads, resistant to weather and

1   This cast iron three-legged pot, now used very effectively as a flower pot, has been cast in a two-piece mould as shown by the vertical seam running from one side to the other. Three-legged pots were the foundation on which the Darbys of Coalbrookdale built their business, but they used a different method of casting.

can be poured into the most intricate of moulds and, most important, it was cheap, would be cheaper and was plentiful — serve to show why cast iron became and remained the most widely used of all metals, until it was superceded by mild steel at the end of the nineteenth century and in more recent times by the widespread use of plastics.

There is hardly any exaggeration in the statement that the Victorians used cast iron for practically everything. Even if 'the iron man cast in his father's mould' is discounted, the list seems endless, although the following will give some idea of the ramifications of the founders' activities. The index to a catalogue issued in the 1890s by a modest general ironfounder lists: tinned, white enamelled and new patent mottled enamelled cast-iron holloware; cast-iron butt hinges of every kind; improved box, flanch and grocer's coffee mills; hat, coat and umbrella stands; door knockers, scrapers and porters. They also made trivets; bar and flat weights for scales; air bricks; Norfolk and stable latches; bell pulls; door knobs and ornamental door hinges. Their manufacturing range included hat, coat and surplice pins; iron and brass frame pulleys; stench traps, and sanitary traps; garden drains and sough grates. In 1836 Archibald Kenrick and Sons, of West Bromwich, published a catalogue with a highly decorative frontispiece listing the items mentioned above together with sad, Italian and box irons; improved sink traps; rice bowls; cast lath and wall nails; shoe bills and pins. As late as 1934 William Cross & Son Ltd offered door porters, boot scrapers, door knockers, trivets, irons and spittoons in addition to their more recently introduced gas cookers and burners.

While coal was replacing wood at the blast furnace it was also becoming more widely used in domestic hearths. As will be seen in the chapter on cooking and keeping warm the change was not without its problems, to the solution of which many great inventors applied their skills, some with success. Eventually, so prolific were designers and so many the manufacturers that the prospective buyer of either a fireplace or a cooker was to be faced with an almost limitless choice from a simple unadorned utility model to a highly ornamental structure in which the primary function of providing heat was subordinate to its architectural features. In architecture too, cast iron found its supporters — and detractors. Macfarlane's catalogue of 1871, mentioned later, is a superb example of the imaginative approach to designing columns, railings, balusters, finials and flag poles, as well as the bandstands, arcades and drinking fountains advertised in later editions. Not only was cast iron important for ornamentation, it was also used in the actual structure of buildings and some, like the Crystal Palace or the Iron Bridge built by Abraham Darby III across the River Severn in Shropshire have received a good deal of publicity. Others have not. Few know that there are at least two churches in Liverpool with cast iron beams, pillars, windows and other parts: St George's, Everton, and St Michael in the Hamlet. Other examples are the Royal Scottish Museum at Edinburgh and the

▲

2 Old catalogues are a fruitful source of information. This page from a William Cross catalogue of about 1934 shows the patented 'Fitzall' trivet — the most mobile of many made by this firm.

Palace of Westminster — the Houses of Parliament — in London. For the latter the designer, Barry, specified galvanised cast iron roof 'tiles' supported by iron beams instead of oak to reduce the risk of a repeat of the fire which destroyed most of the buildings in 1834. Then there was the orangery at Chatsworth House, Derbyshire, designed by Joseph Paxton as the prototype for his Crystal Palace in which the Great Exhibition of 1851 was held.

Among the more unusual uses to which cast iron was put was a bed invented by a Dublin man, Mallet, tobacco pipes, candlesticks, buttons, coffin nails, church pulpits, the earliest cloches called Wardian cases after their inventor, and the morte safe, a Victorian device into which a coffin was put to defeat grave robbers. Then there were garden seats, tables, sundials, ornaments, toys, money banks, mileposts, sign posts, street and other name plates, wall plaques, gutter and manhole covers, public conveniences, notices put up by the authorities, bollards, lamp standards and trade tokens. In the following chapters many of these and other items which could form the basis of a collection of old and ageing cast iron will be dealt with. No mention, however, will be made of cast iron used in industry or agriculture since these appear to be of greater interest to the industrial archaeologist who may have more room in which to arrange and display exhibits.

No finished casting is likely to be the work of one craftsman. Cooperation between the patternmaker, usually a skilled wood-carver who turns an artist's or engineer's design into three dimentional reality, a mould maker and the foundryman are all needed. So too is a finisher who cleans the casting of all its unwanted bits of metal and sand. One cannot work successfully without the others. The pattern, slightly larger than the finished piece since molten iron shrinks about a quarter of an inch per foot as it cools, is used to make a mould using special sand tamped around it and this mould then has to be filled by the foundryman with metal of the correct type and at the right temperature. Each foundry employs these four craftsmen who, taken together with their back-up assistants means that a large undertaking at the end of the nineteenth century could have employed as many as 2,000 men. Ironfounding in Britain spread from the South to Wales, from Wales to the Midlands, then to the North-East and also to the North-West Coast. At an early date it found a foot-hold in Scotland, particularly in the area west of Edinburgh called Falkirk. In that part of the industry alone there were over 6,000 employed in 1880.

Among the hundreds of firms deserving mention for the quality or diversity of their work, four are of particular interest to collectors. Their qualifications for special notice rest either on the fact that they were pioneers or upon the excellence of a particular facet of their production. The fact that they also used trade marks on their products adds to the interest. The Darbys and the company extablished by Abraham Darby, at Coalbrookdale in Shropshire in 1707, have already been mentioned as the pioneers of ironfounding using coal as the fuel for smelting. This firm had a long and distinguished history and is now a division of Allied Iron-

CINDER SIFTERS

ARNOTT SHOVELS.

▲

3   It may seem surprising that these accessories were not made by a stove founder but perhaps they were too small for a large enterprise to be bothered with. In any case Baldwin, Son and Company of Stourport, England, was the maker and the catalogue is dated 1898.

FISH KETTLES.

▲

4   The same catalogue advertised bowls, pans, kettles, pots for almost every use including special kettles for cooking turbot (a kind of fish), ham, glue, tea, coffee, chocolate and even grog. Their tea pots, designed to be held over an open fire by an iron tripod were sometimes called 'Gipsy' pots. See also Fig 195.

N° 2008
Berlin Black 60/
Bronzed 60/
Relieved 80/

6ft 8in high

▲

5 Kenrick made coat, hat and
umbrella stands of which this
is an example. Just under 7 ft high,
they would be difficult to place in
most modern homes.

founders. Their vast two-volume catalogue of 1875 is a revelation of the development of a tremendous range of products, commencing with the three-legged pot-bellied pots for which Abraham Darby developed and patented a casting method giving thinner and tougher articles. They were a popular and cheap replacement for the brass vessels imported from the Continent and in particular, Holland.

Another great name, that of the Carron Company (established in 1759) follows closely on that of Coalbrookdale. Formed by three men from Birmingham, Dr Roebuck a physician, Samuel Garbett a businessman and William Cadell an ironfounder it had, near Falkirk in Scotland, all the ingredients for success near at hand — iron ore, coal limestone and easy access to the sea via the River Carron. Although from the beginning the company concentrated on cannon and grates (the 'Carronade' gun was so reliable it was used extensively by the Royal Navy) the firm helped James Watt in his experiments with the steam engine and also provided railings, gates and balconies for the great architectural developments of the Adam brothers.

Archibald Kenrick and Son (established in 1791) was another respected ironfounder whose head office was and still is in West Bromwich. Their story is one to be admired for overcoming at least two serious crises during their 189 years of business. At first they were brass founders specialising in shoe buckles. In Regency times, however, there was a change in fashion to shoes with laces and as their trade declined they turned first to casting small brass items such as door knockers, ornaments and the like but then became ironfounders, where they established a reputation for the excellence of design and quality of their goods. Iron founding, in its turn, suffered a decline but just in time an Australian inventor, Shepherd by name, who had been trying to sell his idea to firms in the United States and the United Kingdom came to visit them. Although no other firm had shown any interest in this new castor invented by Shepherd, Kenrick saw its advantages and made a success of the venture. The Shepherd castor is now by far the largest part of Kenrick's production and is copied all over the world. Although they are no longer ironfounders, articles with the old Kenrick trade mark are of great interest to collectors of cast iron.

Another name of great import in the foundry trade is that of Falkirk Ironworks. Formed in 1810 by some of the Carron employees during the height of the Peninsular wars against Napoleon and at a time when the trade was booming, Falkirk eventually became the second largest foundry in Scotland, Carron being the largest. Their products were of excellent quality and ranged through the major types such as ornamental items, grates, stoves, smoothing irons and many other utilitarian articles.

Although not as well known as the four important founders mentioned above the firm of Walter Macfarlane & Company of Washington Street and Possil Park, Glasgow, was of some importance in the field of architectural castings. Their products are, however, to be found in many parts of the world and the head of the firm and his castings are described thus in the catalogue of 1871:

> The legitimate development and application of Iron Work have been carefully studied and followed as a profession by our Mr Macfarlane for nearly the last forty years, the earliest portion of that time having been devoted to 'Hammered Iron Work', and the latter to 'Cast Iron Work'. It is to be regretted that so valuable a material as Cast Iron, should occupy the subordinate position it has hitherto done, almost invariably appearing under the borrowed form of some other material, as stone, wood, bronze, &c. That it has a high destiny to fulfil, and is capable of occupying an honest and an honourable position, we think the following pages bear ample testimony. Metals, like men, arrive at perfection through successive stages of refinement, and we must not lose sight of the fact that Cast Iron applied to the decorative arts, is only in its infancy dating no farther back than two or three hundred years, during which time little intelligence had been evinced in realising its power and truthful expression.

▲
6 No records exist to tell us whether this cannon, found in the moat at Caerlaverock Castle, Dumfriesshire, Scotland, was ever fired in anger. But cast iron 'Carronade' made by the Carron Company in Scotland were so reliable that Lord Nelson used them at the Battle of Trafalgar — 21 October 1815 — when the French fleet was decisively routed.

That Walter Macfarlane had pretentions to artistry in ironfounding is clear and his catalogue is an immense collection of line drawings illustrating architectural castings. Some of the designs or ones of similar nature copied by others may be noted on Victorian buildings, but as these are torn down so the ironwork is often lost.

Smelting iron started much later in America than it did on the Continent of Europe or in England for it had to wait until English and Scottish colonists brought their knowledge across the Atlantic. The first furnace appears to have been set up in about 1619 at Jamestown in Virginia but it was overrun within three years by hostile Indians and never restarted. The Pilgrim Fathers who landed near Cape Cod, Massachusetts, realising the need for supplies of iron tools started crude furnaces after they found deposits of bog ore which could be smelted with the readily available charcoal. It is, however, the Saugus Ironworks, established in about 1643 at a site called, appropriately, Hammersmith on the Saugus River about ten miles north of Boston, Massachusetts, which is credited as being the birthplace of the American iron and steel industry. The site, now restored as it appeared in 1650, operated until 1675 when it failed mainly because of a shortage of wood for charcoal. It comprised a blast furnace, a forge, rolling and slitting mills housed in a building reputed to be of oak brought from England. Joseph Jenks (1602-83), an English immigrant, founded the enterprise and catered for the local need for stoves, pots — notably the Saugus pot — pans, nails, hinges, horseshoes and tools. Other achievements were the casting of the dies for the first coins made in America — the pine-tree shilling — and making the first American fireback.

By the middle of the eighteenth century many more undertakings had sprung up as new ore deposits were found in Pensylvania, then Ohio, Indiana and Illinois and during this period the centre of the smelting industry moved into Pennsylvania and later farther west. Although the eastern furnaces did supply munitions

11

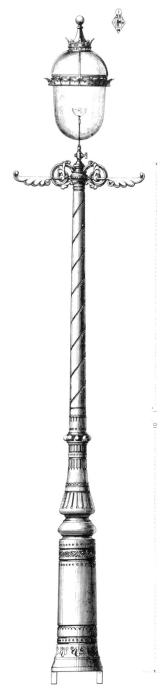

7 One of the many gas street lamp standards illustrated in the fifth edition of Macfarlane's catalogue, dated 1870/1.

for the War of Independence (1775-81) it was these western States that became paramount as the century closed. Among the most famous was the Pennsylvania ironmaster Henry William 'Baron' Stiegel, whose life has been most often documented. Two years after his arrival from Germany in 1750 he was fortunate enough to marry Elizabeth Huber, daughter of a wealthy founder of Brickersville, Lancaster County, Pennsylvania, whose holdings he purchased five years later. This and other acquisitions made him very prosperous, but when in 1762 he built a glass factory which absorbed much of his time and interest his fortunes began to decline. This and his spendthrift habits eventually forced him to become a bankrupt. Some of his castings, including stove plates, are preserved in museums and private collections.

As wood, and thus charcoal, became scarce in Britain, legislation was used to support the foundry industry, resulting in an Act of Parliament of 1750 making it legal for American furnaces only to smelt iron for 'pigs' to be exported to the home country. This, of course, incensed the Colonists and some historians claim the Act was as much as anything else a major contributory cause of the Revolution. In spite of attempts to enforce the law it was much ignored — more and larger furnaces were built, especially in Pennsylvania, to supply finished articles of which stoves are an important example. Remains of furnaces dating from the 1760s have been found, for example, in Virginia and research has shown that contrary to the Act new furnaces were started in the years after 1750. For example the Carlisle Iron Works was started in 1762 at Boiling Springs in The Cumberland Valley of Pennsylvania. It eventually became the property of the Ege family, ironmasters extraordinary of that State. Stiegel, too, in about 1757 is known to have erected a new and larger factory which he called Elizabeth Furnace after his wife. Among other early works was the Marlbro Furnace in Frederick County, Virginia. Here, about 1767, Isaac Zane, a Quaker from Philadelphia, with partners Samuel and John Potts Jr, purchased a furnace started some years earlier by Lewis Stevens. The site was close to good quality ore and trees for charcoal and although, to comply with the law, production was mainly of pig iron for shipment to England there were substantial quantities of pots, kettles, pans, Dutch ovens, flat irons as well as decorative stove plates and firebacks produced.

However, it was after the end of the Civil War (1861-5) that iron founding became big business in the United States and it was deposits of coal allied to those of iron in those States just west of the Eastern Seaboard that were of great importance in assuring the future prosperity of the foundries there. In Britain forty or fifty years were to pass before coke was to become the common fuel for smelting after Abraham Darby succeeded in his experiments, but since wood for charcoal was more readily available in America the change was even slower with the result that it was not until the late 1830s before it became practically complete. When coke was in general use virtually every town with access to the necessary raw materials seems to have had its own furnace producing a wide range of goods for the locality. Eventually some specialisation crept in and Troy, New York, a city at the centre of an effective canal — and later railway — network became famous for its stoves. At one time, according to John G. and Diana S. Waite of the New York State Board for Historic Preservation writing in the magazine *Antiques* in January 1973, there were at least 300 stove makers in operation from time to time between the 1830s and the turn of the century. As the early centre of the US steel industry its fate was sealed by Andrew Carnegie's great undertakings near Pittsburg, built in 1863.

Other iron founders turned to architectural casting and of these one of the most renowned was Hayward, Bartlett & Co of Baltimore, Maryland — later called Bartlett, Robbins in 1866 — by which time they had become established as suppliers of the iron roof to the Norfolk Customs House and the material for the iron building of the New York publishers Harper Brothers. It is stated that they could make all the parts of a building — roof, floor, windows etc, as well as vaults, fences, gates, summer houses, vases and statuary, seats, settees and in addition were also manufacturers of heating and cooking equipment. Some foundries restricted their production to casting decorative gates, railings, balconies and window guards and of these Robert Wood's Ornamental Ironworks of Quaker Ridge Road, Philadelphia gained a reputation as a manufacturer of railings for cemeteries, public and private buildings, verandas, settees, fountains and other ornamental products. Other names mentioned in the literature are Leeds Ironworks and the Shakespeare Ironworks of New Orleans, while E. Graeme and Joan Robertson in their book *Cast Iron Decoration* list not only Lorio Iron Works and Hinderer's Iron Works of New Orleans but also J. L. Mott, 84-90 Beekman St, New York, and Chase Bros, Boston.

In Britain and in America from the mid-1800s until the late-1920s there were hundreds, possibly thousands, of firms engaged for shorter or longer periods in the art — and in those days it was an art — of casting iron, making articles that are now of interest both to the collector and the preservationist. Many, probably most, have not survived as businesses but their names, moulded into so many of their products, are never likely to be completely forgotten. This is particularly true, it appears to the author, of American ironfounders. Here, it seems, almost all small articles and most stoves, bear the name of their maker — although an exception must be made in the case of toys — names so numerous that a comprehensive list has yet to be produced. To a lesser extent the same situation exists in Britain, but either because they were too modest or because extra work was required of the pattern maker one sees many anonymous pieces. On the other hand it does not appear to be possible to pick out any one firm in America as being paramount in its particular field — perhaps they were all first class — but more likely their activities were too short lived to be researched to the extent that Coalbrookdale and Carron have been. Or perhaps they were less extensive in their activities than

Macfarlane or even less renowned than Kenrick for their smaller articles. One wonders whether there ever was a firm in America offering and making as many models of stove, range and heater as did Smith and Wellstood of Bonnybridge, Scotland in its heyday.

It will be clear already that there is a tremendous diversity of items that have been made in cast iron. This book can only illustrate a small selection, but it is hoped that these show the type of objects that are being increasingly collected. Examples are shown from both Europe and America, but it must be emphasised that many designs were very similar, or even identical, on both sides of the Atlantic, and of course most of the large companies exported their products to almost all parts of the world. In these pages emphasis is given to the smaller decorative objects that can be collected and displayed; architectural items cannot be 'collected' in the same way, but are featured so that encouragement is given to their appreciation, preservation and enhancement.

2 *Cast Iron in Architecture*

The Chinese are known to have used cast iron in architecture as early as the tenth century and pagodas ranging from miniature replicas to towers a hundred feet or more high have been found. It was also used instead of bronze for temple equipment such as braziers, censers, caldrons and bells. Although cast iron did not come into widespread use in the Western world until much later, it is known that the railings around St Paul's Cathedral, London were cast in 1714. Robert and James Adam used it extensively in ornamental railings, balconies and gates when designing their great Adelphi development in 1772-4. Nash (1752-1835) also used it for decoration in his plans for Regent Street, Regent's Park and his other London building, when great estates were being broken up to provide accommodation for the increasing urban population. Cast iron did not, however, become really popular with architects until the nineteenth century.

From then until its decline at the turn of the twentieth century no building, and that could include some of the most humble, could be completed without some form of decoration using cast iron. Terminals, finials, crosses, bannerettes, weather vanes and flag staffs all made their contribution to the outward appearance of Victorian residences and public buildings and although fussy they were deemed to be of the best taste. The metal was of course still extensively used for balconies and railings many of which can still be found.

In the past, if a column was desired it was made of stone, marble or wood — the first two very expensive and the third of uncertain durability. If an iron railing was required it was made of wrought iron by a craftsman who needed a great deal of time to finish the work. There was little scope for repetitive manufacture — the last piece needed the same time for completion as the first. With cast iron all was changed. The ironmaster hired a wood carver to create from an artist's drawing a pattern from which duplicate castings could be turned out almost as fast as iron could be melted. No need now to skimp on its use. The customer had only to look at a manufacturer's catalogue to choose what he wanted and the goods could be virtually taken from the shelf. What a boon for those who built on a grand scale and a great benefit even to those small developers who had to please only one or two customers? So great was the variety of designs, too, that unlike ladies' dresses made on a mass production basis, one building was not likely to be exactly like its next door neighbour, decoratively speaking.

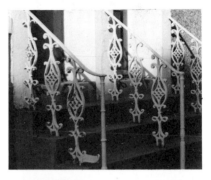

▲
8   Railings of this kind can be found in front of many of the simpler type of terraced home in older parts of cities and towns. Of local manufacture, one type incorporate a boot scraper, essential when streets were unpaved.

15

▲

9 Although modern these balcony railings are interesting because they incorporate the anthemion or honeysuckle motif to produce a pleasing, classical design.

10 The ornate gas lamp holder, date of the building and its name, as well as the finial, are of cast iron. When the railway came to Keswick, Cumbria in the Lake District it brought many tourists for whom this hotel did and still does provide accommodation.

▼

The decoration required by the new style of terrace house with its areas, its doors well above unpaved street level and numerous windows, had a useful function which was in fact its original purpose. Railings and gates were needed to protect gardens and to prevent pedestrians from falling into those basement areas where the servants worked below street level; balustrades were provided to separate entrances from each other and to support those who came up the steps to call or left the house. Balconies provided a place to take the air or show some plants and balconettes acted as guards preventing anyone falling from the long windows fashionable in those days. Simple structures made up of plain castings could have served the practical needs to which these additions were to be put, but this was not good enough for the great architects of the day whose predecessors, Inigo Jones, Sir Christopher Wren and others, had made ornamental additions a popular fashion with those who commissioned their work. Thus we see a deliberate fusion of practicality with, some would say, over-embellishment. With the need to support a balcony, to protect the public or even to provide a means by which rain water could be taken from the roof to the gutters was added a desire to enrich the work. Columns then received 'applied ornamentation', while palmette, acanthus, anthemion and rinceau motifs were used to create railings, gates and balconies and even humble gratings became an intricate example of the skill of the foundryman.

Not everyone approved of cast iron. John Ruskin believed it lacked craftsmanship. Augustus Welby Northmore Pugin (1812-52) declared amongst other things that cast iron was a 'deception, it is seldom or never left as iron. It is disguised by paint either as stone, wood or marble. . . .' There were, of course, those who were active in designing for the new medium such as L. N. Cottingham who published his *The Smith and Founder's Director* in 1824 or Henry Shaw with his *Examples of Ornamental Metal Work* of 1836. Such artists as these were much more restrained than some of those to follow. At a later date some of the large ironfounders began to do their own designing or at least to employ artists who would do it for them. This trend was not altogether successful since the results, while imaginative, were often elaborate and florid. Whether these patterns were the result of changing fashion or whether the founders themselves led the public into a taste for over-ornate casting it is impossible to say. Whatever happened, the results, some of them in a highly baroque style, were often more a credit to the ironfounder's skill than to the artistic judgement of the designer.

Cast decoration of the kind so popular in Victorian Britain was used all over the United States and in many parts of Canada and can be seen both in small towns and large cities. Older and well established areas all have their quota of iron lacework, most of which is cast iron, and it is here where the searcher is most likely to be rewarded. Many sites have already been researched and documented in New York, Boston and the New England States, Philadelphia, Baltimore, Georgetown, Charlestown, New Orleans and San Francisco for example. *Cast Iron Decoration, a world survey* by E. Graeme and John Robertson (Thames and Hudson) is a finely produced book of photographs of some of the most interesting and high quality cast iron used in architecture and it is recommended reading for anyone interested in the subject. American designs were based at first on those of English origin and Cottingham's influence is easily discernible. It seems doubtful whether American artists or craftsmen ever developed their own genre in cast iron although a French influence is said to be seen in parts of New Orleans.

Of the many foundries able to supply architectural items to the building trade in Britain two names are among the most prominent: Coalbrookdale Company of Shropshire and Walter Macfarlane & Company, Saracen Foundry, Glasgow. Study of their old catalogues is a revelation. For example Macfarlane's fifth edition of 1870/1 — there is no date but a presentation copy bears the date 1871 — is a hardback volume weighing about thirteen

11 Grave railings, some of them quite simple in detail, protected grave markers from vandals in both country and city church yards. Compare the simple dignity of this example with the over-ornate railings shown in some of the later illustrations.

12 Macfarlane, in their catalogue of 1870/1, provided the prospective customer with examples of how their products could be used and how they would look on a building.

▼

13 Probably the work of some local founder these railings and brackets used on the Keswick Hotel are an attractive feature.

▼

14 Some founders specialised in architectural iron work on which stairs, stair railings, balusters and newel posts are an important section. Spiral stairs like this offered by Macfarlane could be matched by competitors in the United States and Europe.

15 An example of how a relic from the past should *not* be treated. A cast iron gas-lamp holder with a copper and glass lantern in need of preservation.

pounds, measuring eleven and a half inches by fifteen and has 596 pages illustrating the products of the company in seventeen sections. There are, for good measure, three line drawings of Macfarlane's premises. Choice is astounding. There are 104 pages illustrating gutters alone, 108 showing a total of 208 finials, terminals, crosses and bannerettes, weathervanes and flagstaffs, while 193 pages show the range of railings and gates. One page could have up to a dozen examples of each item. At the end of the catalogue there are twenty-five pages in which their range of public conveniences, all discreetly decorated in an elaborate style, is illustrated. The first decorative iron used on American buildings may have come from abroad but soon there were iron founders ready to supply a local substitute. According to one authority there were 26 foundries making ornamental castings between 1744-1900 (*A Guide to American Trade Catalogues, 1744-1900*). The Robertsons mention The New York Wire Railing Company, and The Architectural Iron Works of the City of New York as important in this field, issuing catalogues of great interest to the researcher. Others have already been mentioned and some of their work can still be identified in New York, Baltimore (Bartlett, Robbins & Co), New Orleans (Hinderer's Iron Works) but much is unmarked and it has not yet been possible to ascribe it to any particular company.

Competition between British companies in the industry was fierce and the battle for supremacy extended even to their catalogues which grew bigger and even bigger, until in 1875 Coalbrookdale published one consisting of two huge volumes from which it was possible to choose anything from the smallest pot to a large public monument. Bandstands, railway stations, houses and even churches — very popular with missionaries because they could be assembled by unskilled labour — were among the architectural treasures in which cast iron was the main material for construction. It had much virtue even in tropical climates where, one thinks, it would have been intolerably hot, for it is termite and rot proof, resistant to weathering and broken pieces could easily be

16 One of Macfarlane's 'Examples' of how their products would look on a building. Here the firm has used just about every opportunity of showing the designer's skill.

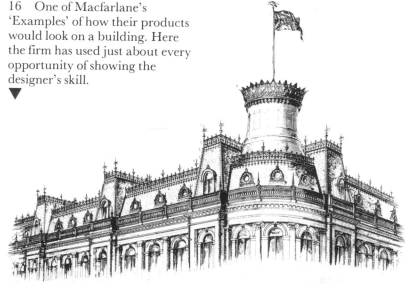

17 Pressure from enlightened individuals has caused Australians to preserve their cast iron 'Lace Work' and houses previously of little interest are now in great demand for renovation. This is one in Melbourne.

18 Here a single piece of 'Lace Work' has been preserved by attaching it to the entrance porch of an Australian home. It is said that the first cast iron was brought as ballast in sailing ships from the United Kingdom.

19 Clients could order a terminal to fit any outline of wall and any particular crest or monogram could be chosen, as shown in this illustration from Macfarlane's catalogue.

20 Ornate lamp standards, first intended for gas, are now often converted to electricity. There is no maker's mark on this good example.

22   Rear gate and railings of St Nicholas Church, Whitehaven, Cumbria, where George Washington's mother lived.

21   Surprisingly, cast iron has been used for the pillars holding up the porch of this small house out in the country. It is believed that the finials, too, are of cast iron as is the knocker.

23   In many North American homes a furnace in the cellar provided much needed heat in the winter. It burned wood or coal and warmed air was conducted to the floor of each room by sheet metal pipes terminating in ornate cast iron covers, like this one, called 'Registers'.

24   A panel from pier railings. The entwined initials — MPCo — are for the Morcambe Pier Company. They alternate with a similar panel which has, instead of the initials, an ivy leaf design.

25   Cast iron ventilators of ornate design were used where there was a possibility of dampness. This is one of a pair over the door to a passage. The pattern shows a desire to lend grace to a very mundane object. Ornate air bricks are, like these ventilators, collectable.

26 Old Cheltenham, Gloucester-shire, England has some of the most graceful iron 'Lace Work'.

replaced by the manufacturer. Its appearance could also be modified by painting to resemble stone or wood. A fair number of public buildings in various parts of the world were constructed entirely, or in a large part, of cast iron and some are mentioned in *Cast Iron Decoration*, eg Smithfield Meat Market, London, the architect for which was Sir Horace Jones; the Coal Exchange, London, designed by J. B. Brunning; the Haughwout Building, New York, built in 1856; Corio Villa, Geelang, Australia and the Banking Premises, Madras, India. Macfarlane, whose buildings were exported to many parts of what was once the British Empire, was proud enough of the Durbar Hall they exported to India to use it as an advertisement in one of their catalogues.

Suddenly the fashion changed, no one now wanted the ornamental decorations so much sought after in Victoria's day, baroque and florid was out and sleek lines were in, fostered by a new generation of architects. On both sides of the Atlantic superb pieces of the best work of the ornamental ironfounder were cheerfully torn down to make way for the new style buildings or to supply scrap for two world wars. Luckily, though much has been lost, many good examples have survived due largely to active preservationists (not local authorities, although even these are now

27 Although this gate in the gardens of Holker Hall, Cumbria, could be wrought iron they seem, on close examination, to be cast. Iron founders could produce surprisingly good imitations of iron that had been shaped by the hammer.

28 Cast iron glazing bars, as seen here at Holker Hall, were used in many Victorian buildings, from stately homes and factories to humble cottages.

29 London's Embankment is decorated with cast iron lamp standards embodying the dolphin, giving weight to the base, as a suitable motif. Cleopatra's Needle is in the background.
Photograph by Brian Jewell, Broadwater Collection Library.

taking an interest). Although one may not appreciate iron decoration it is worth looking at and it can be seen if one keeps one's eyes open when travelling about. Even a visit to a graveyard can be a revelation, for those cast railings surrounding graves and cursed by voluntary grass cutters have a certain charm. In America particularly, grave surrounds are decorated with signs of sorrow or emblems of a life cut off in its prime. The weeping willow, faded lily, popies representing sleep, even inverted torches and laurel wreaths, skulls and cross bones or weeping angels can all be found.

3 Cooking and Keeping Warm

30 A fireback reputed to come from the 'Totsey', the old guild hall which formerly stood at the market cross, Gloucester. It is dated 1661 and bears the coat of arms of the Stuarts according to museum records.

In the beginning the same wood fire, which in northern climates at least occupied a central position in his hut, kept man warm and cooked his food. Later, when he built more pretentious dwellings these, like the hut, had a hole in the roof to let out the smoke, still from a central fire. At first, too, he could cook only by roasting since he had no containers in which to boil and it is probable, too, that huddling together produced as much heat as did the fire which in spite of the outlet in the roof filled the room with smoke. Life on the whole would have been cold, wet, smoke choked and with a very limited menu. Heating conditions in Britain do not seem to have improved until the Normans, who, unlike those before them, preferred to live in two-story buildings, and built their castles in the twelfth century. These castles had to be heated

31 One of the most famous firebacks was cast by Richard Lenard at Brede Fournis, 1636. In addition to the portrait of Richard there are the tools of his trade, a dog and items for household use, which the foundry may have manufactured. The original is in the Every Collection at Lewes, Isle of Wight, and this reproduction can be seen at the Ironbridge Gorge Museum.

32　A fireback which appears to show Adam being offered an apple by Eve, in 'modern' dress. Biblical scenes were common on firebacks.

33　The fireback in Fig 32 as it would be used in an open fireplace with fire dogs, and cast iron pot hanging from a crane.

34　This comes from the Speach House, Forest of Dean and has the arms of Edward VI, 1547. It is in Bishop Hooper's Lodgings, Gloucester.

in the winter no matter how hardy the inhabitants, and this could not be done in the old way. As the floors were of wood on which a fire could not safely be lit it was moved to a wall where a stone platform had been built as the fireplace. These first constructions, like the central fire, had no chimney but they seem to have been more efficient for both cooking and heating than the earlier method. The later development of chimneys, while reducing the nuisance from smoke, brought other problems. For example they had to be cleaned.

As the fire was moved to a wall some protection for the brickwork was required and amongst the most ancient examples of the foundryman's art are firebacks which according to H. R. Schubert's *History of the Iron and Steel Industry in Great Britain* must have originated about the time fires were moved from the centre of the house to the wall, a change which started in the twelfth century and ended in the fifteenth century. The use of a wall fireplace made protection for the bricks and mortar necessary and cast iron

▲
35   The Fleur de Lis and dolphin design betrays a French influence

36   Dog grates were made with baskets so that they would burn coal. Here the ornate fireback depicts what seems to be a fierce battle in Roman times. The grate is to be seen in Sizergh Castle, a National Trust property near Kendal, Cumbria. ▶

37   A hob grate — two boxes, one at either side of the fire. This grate has the added refinement of a fluted reflector at the rear and what might be called 'Adam' decorations. There is also an ash guard or 'tidy Betty' and an ornate fender. ▶

slabs not only provided this but also reflected the heat back into the room, improving the comfort of the occupants. It is believed that the earliest firebacks were plain, but founders soon began to embellish them with simple patterns such as that produced by pressing a rope into the sand of the mould. These crude designs were followed by more elaborate story-telling pictures, which were first carved in wood as a pattern for the sand mould.

Hastings Museum, East Sussex, England, has a large collection of old firebacks or fireplates, one of which shows a man and woman being burned to death at Burwash, also in Sussex, while that illustrated in Fig 31 with the inscription 'Richard Lenard Founder at Brede Fournis' is a well-known example of a commemorative fireback. Raymond Lister, in his book on decorative ironwork mentions other motifs such as armorial bearings, kitchen utensils, animals, birds, plants, armorial signs such as the buckle of the Pelhams, the suns of the Luces and Fourniers, or the Granjon acorn. Other collections of firebacks in England can be found at Anne of Cleves House, Lewes, East Sussex — the Every Collection — Treasurer's House, York, now owned by the National Trust, and the Victoria and Albert Museum, London.

Fireplates, like many other ideas, migrated from the Continent to America with the colonists. It is believed that the first American manufacture took place at Saugus where in 1660 Jenks made one for John and Alice Pickering of Salem, Massachusetts. It was probably made from a pattern imported from England. Indeed it is likely that most were cast using imported patterns or copied from Continental originals. The number of early survivors is comparatively small and most are later than the first quarter of the eighteenth century. Even rarer are firebacks made in Pennsylvania where the design was much influenced by Dutch and German craftsmen.

▲ 38   A bedroom grate with an ornate surround and complete with its fender and fire irons. Wallington House, Northumberland, England. (A National Trust property).

40   Wallington House is preserved as it was many decades ago and the kitchen is a revelation with its great cooking range and array of pots, pans and other equipment.

39   Much attention was paid to detail. Besides the coloured tiles in the alcove this stove has clearly marked pull-out dampers with which to direct the fire into which ever   part was required to be heated. Two ovens, a roaster and a baker were provided, as is an ash guard.

▼

▼

41 A very heavy looking fireplace relieved only by the bright tiles — themselves collectable. There is an integral cast hood over the fire to improve draught.

42 The use of free standing stoves for room heating became popular in the late 1800s. This rather restrained example warms one of the galleries at Wallington House.

43 Perhaps garish is the best description for this grate and overmantel. Except for the tiles and mirror it is all cast iron. The manufacturer's initials, WHM & Co with an R underneath have not yet been connected with any particular firm.

Real advances in better cooking and heating arrangements had to wait for the arrival of good cheap cast iron. This brought reasonably priced cooking utensils and life was revolutionised by the use of coal as a replacement for wood as a source of energy. The old fireplace with accommodation for great billets of oak and seats for people was fine for wood, but when coal was used the room was soon filled with unpleasant fumes. Sooner rather than later someone invented the 'dog' grate with its basket into which the fuel was placed, an adaptation of the fire dogs used for wood. When this was fitted into the old chimney (which was wide enough to hide a friend on the run) it still smoked badly. Later a box or two was added at the side to fill up the space previously occupied by the fireplace. Called a 'hob' grate it too smoked irritatingly.

The smoke problem became so acute as time passed and more coal was used for fuel that some of the most intelligent men of the era — Prince Rupert, Benjamin Franklin and Sir Benjamin Thompson (who later became Count Rumford), among many

44 A very fine fender, in perfect condition and with a restrained motif.

45 Ash guards or 'tidy Betties' as they are also called, are collectable. This, called The Cottage, has much information on the back — the Victorian lozenge showing the design to have been registered 16 August 1880 and Chas Ezard's name, possibly the designer.

46 An ash guard with a nautical flavour. Queen Victoria's profile can be seen centre top. Corrosion has obliterated what may have been the name of the ship.

47 A floral ash guard in good condition.

No. 242 "ELLIPTIC."

No. 285 BACK BOILER.

▲

48 and 49   When coal replaced wood as a fuel 'hob' grates were among the earlier designs intended to use it more satisfactorily. The two boxes on either side at first served only to fill the old wood-burning hearths. They were found to be convenient resting places for pots or pans and later were developed into ovens and water heaters. These grates were made by the Carron Company.

others, made various more-or-less successful attempts to alleviate the nuisance. Their innovatory efforts were assisted very little, and neither was the public, by a lunatic fringe of so-called 'Smoke Doctors' who proposed many, often very impractical, solutions. Among the expedients suggested were such devices as upside down grates which burned from the top downwards; reversible grates to be turned over as fresh fuel was added; drawers which could be pulled out to give more heat when required, and even double fire grates. None worked at all well, because the need to provide a strong draught, which would not only take off the smoke but, equally important, would provide sufficient oxygen for efficient combustion, was not fully understood. It was Count Rumford who, by restricting the base of the chimney flue and by bringing the fire as far forward as possible, went a long way towards making it possible to burn coal in an economical manner and so reduce the amount of smoke produced. It should be realised that smoke represents unburned fuel and that when there is a great deal of smoke then there is waste. Fireplaces which were modified to conform to Count Rumford's principles were said to have been 'Rumfordised'.

The 'hob', however, and a variant called the 'Bath' grate in which a semi-circular casting like a hood partly filled the chimney opening to increase the draught, continued to be popular with the majority into the mid 1800s for two reasons in spite of the fact that they did not fully conform to Rumford's principles. In the first place iron founders had developed a 'Bath' grate that could be delivered to the customer in a 'knocked down' state ready for assembly thus saving transport costs and also it used more iron — an important matter when foundries were short of work. The second reason was that the hob was a convenient place on which to put a pot or a pan, a very popular feature with the busy housewife. Hobs were so much in demand that they were still available in the twentieth century.

For settlers in those parts of the American continent where winters can be long, cold and unpredictable, keeping warm was a matter of life or death, much more so than in England. Enormous wood-burning fireplaces served the first colonists well but they were greatly influenced by ideas for more effective cooking and warming appliances coming from Continental Europe, with its similar extremes of climate. Germans brought the cast iron 'jamb' or 'five plate' stove in about 1740 and shortly thereafter began manufacture in Pennsylvania, where large numbers of them settled. A 'five plate' stove can best be described as a box with one end missing, and placed in the wall between rooms. Warmth from a fire in the closed end of the box heated one room while the open

50   Smith and Wellstood of Bonnybridge, Scotland, advertised this logical evolution of the hob in their catalogue of 1904. Cooking pots could be bought to fit the holes in the stove top where they would be in contact with the hot gases. In the illustration the holes are covered by cast iron lids.

51 Made for export, the 'American Pearl' would burn various fuels. In addition to an oven it has a cupboard in the base where food could be kept warm. It was also a good place to dry kindling and wet shoes (if not left too long).

THE "AMERICAN PEARL" RANGE
(Trade Mark Registered).
WITH HOT CLOSET BASE.

end, under a chimney, warmed the other. Plates, cast separately and bolted together, were decorated with scenes, mainly of a Biblical nature and from German quotations. They were made until 1768 and the Mercer Museum of Bucks County Historical Society, Doylestown, Pennsylvania houses a large number. By adding a front plate, with a fuel door and draft hole, the 'five plate' stove became the 'six plate' or 'Holland' stove. It was brought to America by Pilgrims who had been living as exiles in the Low Countries. After about 1800 they became known as 'box' stoves and while additions and improvements were added from time to time they continued to be popular for many years. A 'ten plate' stove had an internal oven consisting of four thin plates placed so the fire surrounded them. These stoves all featured highly ornamental decorations in the German manner, and for further information on early examples *The Bible in Iron or Pictured Stove Plates of the Pennsylvania Germans* by Dr Henry C. Mercer should be consulted. First published in 1914 it was reprinted in 1961. Stove plates cast from the second quarter of the nineteenth century adopted flower and fruit detail based on Greek scenes or classical motifs for decoration. Running concurrently with the evolution of the 'box' stove was that of the 'Franklin' stove another kind of room warmer invented by Benjamin Franklin in 1742. This was really a sophisticated fireplace filler created specifically to burn coal. The story of its invention and subsequent development has frequently been told and need not be repeated here.

At some time in the early 1800s a more or less complete separation of the functions of grates and stoves into those for cooking only and those for heating seems to have taken place. For cooking, both the hob and the 'box' stove had additions of an oven and a tank for heating water as well as many inventions intended to improve efficiency. Decoration, too, became a 'selling point' and the more elaborate the castings and the brighter the decorations the better. A purchaser could choose from an enormous selection just what suited his or her taste or purse. Although popular in Britain 'built in' ranges such as Carron's 'Lancashire' were less so in America although they did have their adherents. Efficiency in the earliest of these ranges was low but was improved by arrangements for conducting heat around the oven and water heater by a series of baffles operated by levers. Free standing cooking stoves were used much more in America where its origins can be traced back to the 'box'. Perhaps the most often seen was a high back type and many of these are still used with satisfaction in rural areas.

In Great Britain open fires were still used for heating until after World War II and in some places even later. Each room had its own

52 A collectable oven door marked Ralph Yates, Malton (Yorkshire), with holes in the facia for the damper rods used to change the direction of heat flow.

53 Parlour stove intended to burn wood. Maker unknown but probably Canadian.

54 A typical kitchen range with a hob on the right and two ovens on the left. Knobs attached to the damper controls are visible above the very fine top oven door.

55 Still in use in an hotel in Darjeeling, India, this old stove is known to be at least eighty years old and may even be one hundred. Probably made in Britain.

fireplace and chimney inevitably producing draughts and fogs and a typical bedroom fireplace of the mid-1800s is illustrated. Ornate and much more elaborate structures were to be found in living rooms. Pictorial tiles, now themselves very collectable, added heat reflection and beauty. Although it was so popular the open fire was known to be most uneconomical and the cause of the great city fogs of the day. As coal became more expensive and servants scarcer the slow combustion stove made its appearance. These free standing stoves do not seem to have been the success they should have been, even though designers catered for a human desire to see the fire by providing doors which could be opened at will to expose the flames. They are now being revived and modern copies can be bought, some cast by the original manufacturer, Smith and Wellstood. North Americans also used room heaters and these were, in the main based on the 'box' stove although some were heavily disguised. However room heating in the northern States developed differently, going into the cellar, and the furnace became a standard method. Hot air was conducted to each room by a series of tin ducts which ended in a cast iron register in the

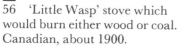

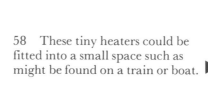

57 'Gold Star' kerosene stove dated 1881 and made by Myers Osborn & Company, Cleveland, Ohio.

58 These tiny heaters could be fitted into a small space such as might be found on a train or boat.

56 'Little Wasp' stove which would burn either wood or coal. Canadian, about 1900.

59 Two American room heaters. The one on the right is made by Granger Bros, Pitsford and that on the left, the 'Charter Oak' probably by C. F. Finely Company, St Louis. See also Fig 68.

60   To increase output from room heaters the smoke was ducted through two sheet metal pipes to the box above and from there to the chimney. Although essentially for space heating this and many others of the type had a place for a pot or kettle between the pillars.

61   A more ornate example of a 'two pillar' stove.

62   In the cold climates encountered in northern United States and Canada stoves served a dual purpose of cooking and heating. This 'Prince Albert' stove, made in 1871 by Horatio Horskin of Bedford, Quebec, Canada, has a large box-like structure at the back which is an oven. It bears Queen Victoria's Arms, as Bedford was settled by a group of United Empire Loyalists.

63 The 'Pandora' stove made by McClary of London, Ontario, Canada, bakes, heats water and has plenty of space on the hot top for boiling and frying. Two hinged shelves on the back support things in need of warmth, while plates and other items can be kept hot in the large warmer above. Said to be eighty years old, it is still in use.

64 Known as the 'Mayflower' from the ships on the side or a 'Cape Cod' because it was used on fishing schooners this three-legged stove is marked 'Tyson Furnace — 1839 — Plymouth, Vermont'.

65 A large version of the 'Wasp' stove. Each had an all-purpose tool for lifting hot stove lids, moving dampers and poking the fire.

floor of the room where the heat was wanted. The writer remembers shovelling tons of coal into what seemed to be the mouth of Hell so that the house could be kept warm during a Canadian winter. Much research needs to be done into the subject of stoves and heaters on both sides of the Atlantic but as a start there is an excellent article on stoves in the recent issue of *Encyclopaedia Americana*.

In the days when a log fire was laid in the centre of the room in a circle of stones or on a low stone platform on a stone floor the need to protect the surrounding area from hot embers which might fall from the cast iron firedogs was minimal, for they could be kicked back into place and no harm was done. As soon, however, as the dog grate was brought onto the scene, and even more so when the hob became ubiquitous, some means of preventing live lumps of coal from escaping onto the wooden floor or the precious carpet. became desirable and the ironfounder was pleased to provide a solution by inventing the fender, or as some call it, the curb. These three-sided barriers placed in front of the fire were often very elaborate castings using architectural and other motifs as a basis for their design. Some took the form of railings, others had rather florid curves and still others were reminiscent of castles. Next came the ash guard or 'tidy Betty' to stand just in front of the grate, behind the fender, to conceal untidy heaps of ash accumulating beneath the fire basket as the coal burned to ash. The ash guard also helped to regulate the draught and keep down dust as the fire was poked to make it burn brighter. They, too, were usually ornate castings, making them very collectable, but they seem to have had different sources of artistic inspiration, perhaps because of their square shape as opposed to the elongated shape of the fender.

Householders were, as has been noted, reluctant to forgo hob grates because of their convenience and because they had a sentimental appeal, but when at last the efficiency of the new models had been demonstrated, and the much higher prices for fuel had been considered, they had to go, and so regional varieties such as the *Lancashire*, *Yorkshire*, *Durham* and other such names could no longer be found in ironfounders' catalogues. Again, in order to placate those who preferred their food cooked in the open and their tea brewed on the open fire, the ironfounder found an answer with the grate trivet. This was merely a bracket made with three lugs placed in such a way that it could be hung on the fire bars close to the fire to form a little shelf. Pots, kettles and tea pots

66 The rail on which customers could rest their feet made these stoves popular in village stores in the USA and Canada. This is called 'Round Oak' No 20 and was made by P. D. Beckwith, Michigan and is dated 1894.

68 Exquisitely made miniature cooking range cast by C. F. Finely Company, St Louis, to demonstrate and take orders for the 'New Charter Oak' stove with a patent hot air flue, 1873. See Fig 59.

67 Moffat Stove Company of Weston, Ontario, still makes stoves and the 'Crown Pearl' was one of its earlier products. The sad irons rest on a removable shelf below, which is itself collectable.

69 Another design for a stove intended for confined spaces. The ledge around the middle on which flat irons could be placed indicates that it is a laundry stove.

could then sit in the glow from the heat of the coals. With one, two or even three trivets one could still have the doubtful advantages of the hob but with a better fire and less smoke.

Trivets are eminently collectable. They were made in hundreds of patterns by a large number of firms and there must have been hundreds of thousands produced. Much skill and ingenuity was lavished on their construction; some had handles, others slid toward or away from the fire to regulate the heat and like one called the *Fitzall* produced by William Cross, some were designed to fit not only barless grates but were adjustable too. The horseshoe enclosing either a five bar gate, a horse's head or a fox mask were among the best sellers, but many very elaborate patterns could be obtained.

Toast, kettle or hearth stands, too, are collectable and they also come in a wide variety of shapes and models. Made to stand in front of the open fire on three or four legs they could support any food that was placed upon them and as they could be moved to any desired spot the correct temperature could be maintained. Some, like the *Justryte* (made by Cross) could be raised or lowered as required. Other items for use with an open fire were of cast iron, such as fire iron rests needed to keep dirty pokers, tongs and shovels off the hearth and in a neat state, all of which are very collectable. Perhaps shovels and sifters do not have the same appeal as the more ornate trivets and hearth stands, but they are all fast disappearing and should make an interesting collection.

Not all stoves were for domestic cooking and heating and those for specialised uses deserve some attention. There were stoves for most trades from laundries to tailors. Even tin-smiths had their special models and a whole range was manufactured for yachts, ships, cabooses at the ends of trains in America, guard's vans, seamstress' workrooms and even harness rooms. They were given evocative names such as *Big Ben*, *Old Ben*, and *Wee Ben*; *Little Dorrit* for tailors and dressmakers; *Jockey* for the harness room or *Watchful* for the guard's van. There is no need to describe the use to which stoves with names like *Pacific*, *Mermaid*, *Spanker*, *Jack Tar*, *Skipper* or *Anchor* were put, it seems rather self-evident.

With the advent of the twentieth century both heating and cooking by gas was advancing rapidly as a replacement for solid fuel, although this new source of heat was still regarded with some suspicion. So much so that Carron made solid fuel cookers with gas as an added extra on a few of their models — rather like the old steam ships which still had masts and sails. Thus, while the majority of their products were of a conventional nature they offered gas grills, ovens or hot plates which could be attached. Later still electricity was in general use but oil as a source of energy came even later.

70 A page from the old catalogue (in the library of the Ironbridge Gorge Museum) of an unknown maker of iron castings showing the range of fire iron rests, few of which seem to have survived. Berlin Black was more durable but less bright than Japanned Black, while electro bronzing was a method of making iron look like brass.

BEATRICE

HEARTH OR KETTLE STANDS.

FINISHED IN ART BLACK, ANTIQUE COPPER OR NICKEL PLATED.

No. 1802.
Size 5¼-in. dia. × 3¾-in. high.
Boxed ¼ Dozens.

No. 1808.
Size 8½-in. × 5-in. × 4¼-in. high.
Boxed ¼ Dozens.

No. 2542.
Size 12-in. × 6½-in. × 6-in. high.

THE "JUSTRYTE" ADJUSTABLE HEARTH STAND.

For use with Gas and Electric Fires.

Fits close against the front of the fire whether square or rounded.
Instantly adjustable and suits any size.
Height, 4¼ inches to 6½ inches.

ART BLACK
COPPER OXIDIZED
ELECTRO BRASSED
CHROMIUM PLATED

71   Beatrice was the trade name of John Harper and the page is from their catalogue of about 1932. The firm, later taken over by Archibald Kenrick, were founders at Albion Works, Willenhall, Staffordshire, England.

73   A fine iron three legged stand about 18in high.

72   William Cross in their catalogue show that they were aware of the coming popularity of gas and electricity and have designed a special trivet or hearth stand. They were fighting a losing battle against new customs which would make the hearth redundant.

74   A trivet for the bars of a hob grate, forming a shelf to support and heat cooking pots, etc. Made by Carron Company, the design was registered 8 March 1879.

75   This 'Good Luck' trivet has the registration number 5509.

76 This trivet, for the Scottish trade, is numbered 2763.

77 Two trivets from the author's collection. On neither is there a clue as to the maker.

Nos. 655—660.
4 Sizes.
With Door and Base Plate, complete with Pan and Grid.

No. 652.
No. 652. One Size only.
11½in. wide × 10in. deep × 9in. high.
With Door and Base Plate, complete with Pan and Grid.

PORTABLE GAS FIRES
THE "CHARMA."

No. 745.

No. 745. Five Radiants.

Extra Radiant Free.

Height 12 inches.

Reversible Burner, Air Regulator, Adjustable Hot Air Ventilator at Top, Fire Brick Back.

IN STOVE BLACK FINISH ONLY.

Each Packed in strong Cardboard Box.

TAILORS' GAS STOVES.

No. 111.

Will heat Tailors' Irons (up to 16 lbs) ready for use in ten minutes.

No. 111. Without Hood.

Extreme size: Length, 14½in.; Width, 5in.
Size at Top: Length, 10½in.; Width, 5in.

No. 112. As No. 111 but with Movable Hood.

Size of Hood: Length, 10in.; Width, 4½in.

78 One supposes that this mark denoted great durability, good finish and low price, but it is hardly a trade mark that one could register. William Cross was the maker.

79 William Cross's catalogue of about 1934 shows that gas was making its mark both in the home and in industry as a source of heat.

4 Clean, Neat and Wholesome

Cleanliness and cast iron were inseparable companions. Cheap iron pipes made it possible to provide economically a public water-supply, which, with sewage disposal installations became commonplace in the late 1800s. There were of course still many, particularly rural, areas without either of these amenities which are today regarded as essential and taken for granted, but even they were to have the benefit of cast iron pumps with which to draw water from the well. In towns and cities throughout the country general health was greatly improved when the new means of keeping clean were made readily available. Not that the change came easily. In many urban situations there were those who would not concede that filth bred disease and disease begat poverty, and they fought to prevent what they termed a waste of public money on unnecessary novelties. They were, however, forced by a report from a commission set up in 1846, to inquire into public health. Sponsored by Edwin Chadwick, it showed how inadequate refuse disposal, inadequate water supplies and bad drainage were largely responsible for cholera and other epidemic diseases.

The report led to the so called 'Health of Towns Act' of 1848, only three years before Queen Victoria opened the Great Exhibition of the Works of All Nations. As the result of the act Local Boards of Health were formed and they began to drag sewage disposal out of its mediaeval state. Prior to the Act and to some later legislation, expecially that made during Disraeli's Conservative Government of 1874-80, control of the sanitary arrangements were in the hands of well-meaning citizens with very little power to compel offenders to keep streets and alleys clean. In one northern English town there was a committee of twelve called the 'Nuisance Removal Committee' whose sole employee, the Sanitary Inspector, was paid five shillings per week and instructed to buy lime and whitewash brushes to lend to poor people to whitewash their houses. Once Local Boards of Health began work demand for miles of cast iron pipe and all sorts of ancillary equipment began to spring up. This was of great benefit to the foundries whose designers soon turned their attention towards making life for the lucky customers of pure mains water even more comfortable. On the other hand, without cast iron, these benefits would have been denied to all but the very rich.

On 8 April 1857 Walter Macfarlane of Saracen Foundry, Glasgow, read a paper before the Philosophical Society of Glasgow, the title of which was 'Sanitary Arrangements, for converting

▲
80 Hand pumps of this kind were essential in every farm yard until mains water became available to most of the population. In the past they were justly accused of spreading typhoid fever because wells were often contminated by seepage from the farm midden.

81 Now ornamental, and collectable, this pump once supplied the water for a nearby house. The lion is similar to that in the previous illustration, it is numbered 46571 but the maker's name is illegible. It has a different handle, too.

82 This is the kind of pump that might have been beside the sink in a farm kitchen or in a home in a village. The author remembers that these were still in use in rural Canada not more than forty years ago.

the excrementary refuse, dry garbage, Ashes &c., of Towns into their proper and most valuable purposes', a subject he quite rightly says 'may not be of the most inviting nature...' but was very necessary. He dealt first with the existing but very unsatisfactory, even primitive, arrangements in Glasgow and followed with his solution comprising provision of improved water-closets, public conveniences and, most important, made the suggestion that surface water only should be allowed to drain into rivers through existing sewers, while foul drainage should be intercepted, taken off by a second sewage system and treated. Of course a good deal of cast iron would be needed in cleaning up a city the size of Glasgow and his hope obviously was that it would be his iron, but even so one must sympathise with his invitation to 'the public generally, and Boards of Health and Municipal Authorities in particular to the prosecution and speedy accomplishment of this important sanitary reform'. His castings for this type of work are hardly collectable and are very unexciting merely because of their subject matter, but Walter Macfarlane was also very keen on providing the public with suitable conveniences, again as a means of using cast iron. Figure 83 shows one of the installations suggested by that worthy sanitarian. Perhaps they are not collectable but they are most certainly preservable.

Among some of the earlier amenities arising from a public water supply was the public drinking fountain. This was probably one of the first means of getting water to the masses. The urban population was particularly favoured although there were those erected in villages, too. Dogs, horses and cattle were also the beneficiaries, since facilities for their refreshment were often incorporated in the design. Although some fountains were of a simple nature others such as those illustrated were very ornate indeed. A prominent feature of all the fountains of the time seems to have been a cast iron cup attached to the fountain by a chain to prevent theft and this, if used extensively must have contributed greatly to the spread of disease. This kind of drinking fountain would hardly be tolerated by public health authorities today but they were still being advertised for sale in 1914, five years before the Local Boards of Health became the Ministry of Health. Although no doubt the majority of fountains were erected to dispense water to the thirsting populace as a first objective they quickly became objects of agrandisement or commemoration. For example, many were put up to commemorate some great event such as Queen Victoria's Jubilees, or as a tribute to some lover of animals and even to preserve the memory of the name of a local worthy in place of a statue. They were also popular overseas and many were exported to what was at one time known as the Empire where they may still stand as tributes to Victorian enterprise.

There can be no doubt that cast iron was the major factor in making bathing a habit and the bath a household convenience. Carron Company is reputed to have introduced it to the British and exhibited one at the 1851 exhibition. One model advertised in 1926 is illustrated and this shows how far bath design has come since that time. As keeping clean became cheaper and less difficult so the ironfounders designed and made other lavatory equipment, some of it quite ornate, as an adjunct to the home, hotel or institution. To show just how eager the ironfounder was to sell his output and how much he was on the look-out for every possible use for his skills one has only to look at figure 91. No doubt cast iron toilet mirrors seem a trifle unnecessary but they were available in the first quarter of this century.

In the business of washing in the home, traditionally a preserve of the dolly tub and the 'posser', ironfounders do not seem to have made any dramatic inroads although a good deal of iron was used in the early washing machines. Iron's main impact — if the word is correct for this context — was in wringing and smoothing. For example, mangles, now collectors' items, were among the early means of pressing water out of clothes and even of ironing flat pieces. Some of those used for ironing had a linen sheet which was wound around the roller. Although it is only recently that mangles have become of interest to collectors other forms of ironing equipment have been sought after for many years and there is even a collectors' club with its headquarters in Paris. As has been stated it was in the smoothing of cloth, clothes and all sorts of other articles that the ironfounder discovered a great source of revenue.

Spinning and weaving are among the earliest industries created by man and a need for smoothing the products of the loom must soon have been recognised. When and where and even how the primitive weaver first found a means of preparing the surface of cloth is unknown but there is a belief that the first means was by use of smooth stones, hot pans and even boards and as usual the Chinese are credited with being among the vanguard. However, for our purposes the first crude 'irons', as they are now known, were made of a lump of metal to which was attached a long metal handle. These were called 'Geese' and are supposed to have been first used by tailors. Somewhat later the ironfounders started to make what we now recognise as the 'iron' and it can only be due to his efforts that 'ironing' became a common type of drudgery. The founders had a two pronged attack on the leisure of the average housewife for not only did they make irons cheap and easy to come by but at the same time assisted materially in the mechanisation of the textile industry, so making cloth much less expensive and thus giving people more power to purchase more clothes, so giving more washing to do and more ironing to get through. In the end of course he sold more irons and at the time of the Great Exhibition of 1851 there were three types of smoothing iron available to the householder who would, no doubt, purchase that most suited to the purse. Cheapest of all were the early 'sad' irons whose price depended on weight and were in fact sometimes in the early days priced at so much per pound. Their weight could range from four to twenty pounds per pair and these lumps of cast iron into which a wrought iron handle had been set during the casting operation are said to have taken the name from an old English word meaning heavy. Hence also a 'sad' cake.

83   Walter Macfarlane offered several types and sizes of cast iron public convenience in the late 1800s of which this is one. The line drawings are so detailed that if one wished now to reconstruct such an edifice it would be quite possible.

84   Drinking fountains were common-place in cities and towns all over the world. They seem mostly to have disappeared and those remaining are seldom in working order.

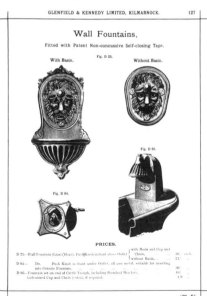

Wall Fountains,

Fitted with Patent Non-concussive Self-closing Taps.

Fig. D 25.

With Basin.　　　　　　Without Basin.

Fig. D 86.

Fig. D 84.

PRICES.

85 and 86 Drinking fountains by Macfarlane, (*top*) and Glenfield & Kennedy (*bottom*).

In no time at all these irons, which were originally rectangular like the billiard table iron, acquired a more or less pointed front end and a blunt back on which they could be rested. At first they were heated in front of the open fire either on the hearth or on a trivet where the handle would get as hot as the iron itself. For laundries, either domestic, industrial or institutional, special stoves for heating irons were made. Protection for the hands came in several ways. First there was Sylvester's patent where a loose barrel handle provided some insulation from the heat of the iron itself. Then there was the wooden handle which was cooler because wood does not act as a conductor of heat. The most successful and most imitated was that of Mrs Potts whose *Enterprise* was patented in the USA in 1871. *Enterprise* was known as a cold handled iron since the handle was not permanently attached to the iron itself. In fact there were usually three irons for one handle, two being heated while the third was in use. The handle was of wood which helped to keep the ironer's hand cool. This iron was also made in Britain by Kenrick and other founders, but the most usual modification to be seen is really a slug iron with a wooden handle that was attached to the lid of the box in which the hot slug was deposited.

There was the obvious risk when an iron was heated, either by the fire or on a special stove, that the iron would be dirty and the dirt transferred to the cloth on which it was used. To reduce the danger a 'slipper' was invented, which could be put over the iron after it was heated, but this was not very popular. By far the most acceptable method of keeping the iron clean involved not the heating of the iron but a piece of cast iron the same shape, which when hot could be slipped into a 'box' with a handle — hence the name 'box' iron. Several metal 'slugs' or as they were often called 'heaters' were provided for each iron so there was a continuous supply of hot inserts which were taken out and replaced with tongs. These box irons were certainly more satisfactory than sad irons, but they were not the last word by any means. The next step was a true self heating model in which charcoal was burned in the body of the iron to produce the right degree of heat. They all had a little spout or funnel at the top to take away fumes and sometimes this could be moved in order that the smoke could be directed in the best position to suit the ironer. They could be kept alight it is said by swinging them over the head but other models had a bellows which fanned the flame in a much safer way. There was also the *Dalli*, invented in Germany in about 1900 and later manufactured in Britain by William Cross and others, which used a charcoal brickette as a fuel and this must have been cleaner and easier to use. Another and later self heating iron used kerosene, and yet another used methylated spirit, but both seem not to have been popular, possibly because of the danger of fire or explosion.

In the late 1800s and early 1900s irons heated by gas became very popular and have only recently gone out of use by a minority of senior citizens, in favour of electricity. Finally indeed there came electricity which, at first, was used to heat irons based on the

87 This fountain at Allanton by Duns, Berwickshire, Scotland, is now unusable. Dated 1875, it may have formed part of a village improvement programe started by the owners of the village in that year, the Housten-Boswell family. It is preserved largely through the persuasion of a local collector of cast iron.

88 Another unusable fountain, this time in Lowther Street, Whitehaven, Cumbria; it bears the arms of the Lowther family and is dated 1859. Provision for animals to drink was not unusual. ▶

89 From the catalogue of Samuel Gratrix Jr and Brother dated 1926, this bath and shower suite must have been the very latest and most fashionable thing in its time.

Iron Lavatory Stands.

90 Gratrix also offered other equipment for keeping clean such as a double ended bath, a lady's lavatory and this iron lavatory stand.

91 Iron framed mirrors like this were priced competitively with those with wood frames.

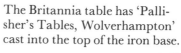

▲
92   An old clothes washer with a good deal of cast iron in it. The 'Patent Ewbank Folding Handle' made the massive machine slightly easier to stow away.

▲
93   Some people collect mangles and these two are in a garden — about the only suitable place for them. On the right is The Crown No 5, made by Joseph Hillary, Aspatria, and on the left one made by J. Branthwaite, Windermere.

The Britannia table has 'Pallisher's Tables, Wolverhampton' cast into the top of the iron base.

▲
94   A large laundry stove showing how 'sad' irons were heated. At least twenty could be placed along the sides and on the top. Two tailor's irons hang on the side and on the top left there is an iron with a 'shoe' to keep it clean while being heated. There are a variety of 'cool' handles on display.

▲
95   Carron made laundry stoves of which this is one. Forty-eight irons and several fluting or quilling tongs — those scissor-like handles protruding from the side — could be heated at one time.

96 Four sad irons for domestic use. From left to right they are marked: JDB 7; T. Sheldon & Co, W-hampton; 5 Sylvester's Patent; and Salter above a knotted rope which surrounds an arrow and the letter S (Salter's trade mark). Number four is similar to number two. 1, 2 and 4 have tubular handles and 3 has the loose 'Sylvester's Patent' handle.

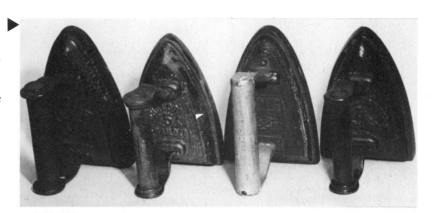

97 William Cross 'Lyng' pattern heater iron with extra heaters. The wooden handle and a metal shield, like the hand-guard on a sword, were of help in keeping the user's hand cool. In the case of this iron, heaters were inserted from the top and not from the end as in earlier models.

98 A typical 'slug' or heater iron with wood handle. Clearly shown at the rear is the trap through which the red-hot heater was inserted.

29

THE "LYNG" HEATER BOX IRON.

WITH NEW IMPROVED LEVER FASTENING.

Each Iron packed in strong Cardboard Box.

BODIES
HIGHLY
POLISHED.

TOPS
JAPANNED
AND GILT.

No. 86.

Fitted with Brass Guards and supplied with our latest Improved Registered Lever Fastener which keeps the top perfectly secure. The Iron can be freely used without any possibility of its coming loose. Complete with Lifter and 2 Heaters. Sizes: 5, 5½, 6, 6½ inch.

EXTRA HEATERS FOR ABOVE.

No. 88.

STATE SIZE OF IRON WHEN ORDERING.

HEATERS FOR OLD PATTERN FINE CAST BOX IRONS.

MADE IN SIZES TO SUIT ALL IRONS.

No. 405.

99 The Dalli, made in Germany about 1900 and intended for use with a charcoal briquette. Ventilation holes promoted combustion.

THE "TOZOT" HEATER BOX IRON.
(Mrs. POTTS' PATTERN).

Complete with 2 standard pattern Heaters and Lifter.

Length from Toe to Toe, 7-in.; Weight, 5¼-lb.

Each Iron packed separately in strong carton.

100 A William Cross iron with an evocative name. This example is very similar to the Kenrick iron in the next illustration. Although called a Mrs Potts pattern it is warmed by a heater inserted from the top, while a true Potts pattern was a handle that gripped a hot base.

101 Kenrick and many others made this type of iron, really a heater iron as the top is hinged to allow insertion of the heater.

▲
102 Charcoal iron with a moveable chimney by William Cross.

▲
103 This is a different type of charcoal iron by the same maker. It has no chimney as there is a damper fitted to the back. One of Cross's trade marks was a Maltese cross.

104 Two children's toy irons of American manufacture. That on the left was made by the Swan Company. ▶

older box or gas type and thus were of cast iron. (They are now of cast aluminium.) When first introduced the electric iron was, like the motor car, subject to some ridicule and one story, no doubt apocryphal, credits laundry maids with continuing to heat the iron on the stove in addition to plugging it into the mains.

So far no mention has been made of irons used by tradesmen and in industry but they, too, are collectable and some of these are to be seen in various museums. The tailor's iron was still known by its old name of 'goose' although it had acquired a conventional handle long ago. These irons could weigh as much as twenty-eight pounds each and must have been very hard work when in use. Hatters, too, had their irons as did laundries — the ones used in the latter were of course similar to those used in the home. One particularly interesting type of smoothing instrument and one of great value to collectors is that called variously Italian or *Tally* iron or less correctly a goffering iron. These are said to have been invented in Italy in the early part of the sixteenth century when ruffs and neck-frills were the height of fashion and some means of keeping them smooth was required. They were also found to be very useful by Victorian housewives whose laundry tasks would have included many articles with frills and ruffles. Some, and these are the most attractive, have brass barrels on iron stands while others were of cast iron. In any case the heater was of iron. It would seem that no home could be complete without a variety of specialist irons such as the ball, egg and mushroom for smoothing particularly difficult work.

Another collectable article connected with the tedious task of ironing is the iron stand. These are attractive because they not only were cast in various quite ornate patterns but they also often had the maker's trade mark incorporated in the design, the study of which can be of enthralling interest leading to the discovery of ironfounders long since taken over, bankrupt or gone out of business for other reasons. A few of the many hundreds of kinds of iron stand sold during the 1800s and 1900s are illustrated.

No doubt it is true that many of the objects described in this chapter are heavy and unwieldy and some could be termed, and with truth, very ugly. Many are too bulky to be of interest as collectors' items to the amateur who is unlikely to have the space in

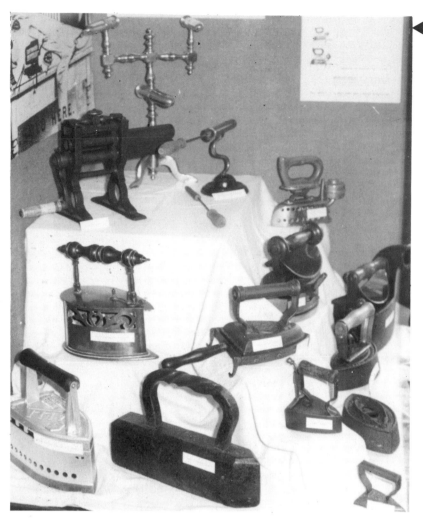

105   In this illustration can be seen a brass 'Tally' iron, crimping rollers, a nickel plated spirit iron, charcoal and sad irons and a real Mrs Potts pattern.

106   A charcoal iron with fixed smoke outlet, wood handle and the curved heat guard, all of which could be removed from the base to add more fuel by releasing the latch.

which to store such items as a public convenience. On the other hand a drinking fountain could find a place in some of the larger gardens while an old pump can sometimes be seen beside a house as an ornamental object. Not many collectors will have a place for an old bath or shower and mangles are not to everyone's taste. But all these objects are as worthwhile preserving as pieces of social history as many items now considered more attractive and interesting. It would be a great loss if some of these original pieces of cast iron were not preserved from the scrap yard, for they can show the next generation where those amenities they take for granted originated. They should at least command the attention of the professional preservationist either in exhibits devoted to social history or less specialised museums like the folk museums now busy exhibiting items from an earlier period.

107   This is a real Mrs Potts pattern iron. It was made in Guelph, Ontario, Canada.

Ball Iron,
with Loose Pillar
and Oval Top.

Ball Iron,
with Loose Pillar
and Round Top.

Mushroom Iron,
with Loose Pillar.

Light Italian Iron.

Piping Iron

Scotch Box Iron.

Best Box Iron.

Mrs. Pott's Box Iron.

Gas Iron.

"Carolina" Charcoal
Box Iron,
Straight Pipe.

"Carolina" Charcoal
Box Iron,
Bent Pipe

Charcoal Box Iron,
No. 800.

Spirit Iron.

Electric Iron, with Stand

Bayonet Cap Attachment and
Flexible Wire.

"Bonus" Petrol Iron.

108   This page from Kenrick's
catalogue of 1926 shows the transi-
tion from solid fuel irons to cleaner
forms of heating. The petrol iron
seems to be intrinsically
dangerous.

109　Two spirit irons and a gas iron, all of American manufacture.

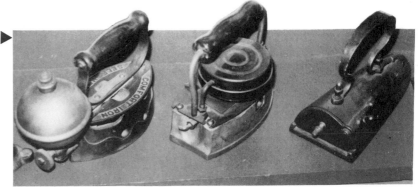

110　Starched linen and cotton ribbons etc were given a crimp ('gauffered') when they were passed between the two rollers which were heated by metal poker-like objects. Bishop Hooper's Lodgings.

111　A crimping iron with a fixed base and a moveable roller.

112　This is a peculiar type of gas iron. One suggestion is that the reservoir on the right was filled with gas, the gas line removed and ironing carried out without hindrance.

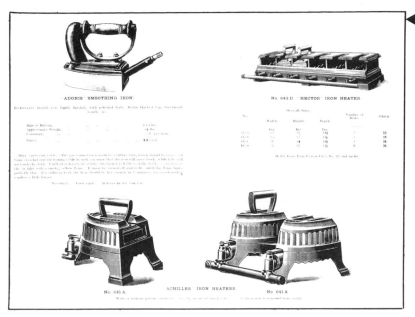

ADONIS SMOOTHING IRON.

No. 643 D "HECTOR" IRON HEATER

No. 641 A   ACHILLES IRON HEATERS   No. 641 A

113   Gas irons and gas iron heaters from the early part of the century. Carron Company catalogue.

114   Gas irons were still popular as late as the 1930s. This example, from the author's collection, is still in usable condition. As can be seen, town gas was fed through the left-hand inlet. Inside is an iron-shaped gas ring. In use gas was turned on, a match applied to one or other of the openings, there would be a 'pop' as the gas ignited and ironing could start as soon as enough heat had been generated.

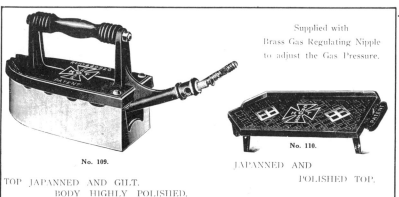

Supplied with Brass Gas Regulating Nipple to adjust the Gas Pressure.

No. 109.
TOP JAPANNED AND GILT.
BODY HIGHLY POLISHED.

No. 110.
JAPANNED AND POLISHED TOP.

115   Tailor's irons used a good deal of metal since they could weigh 18 lb and they were also tiring to use. William Cross's Maltese Cross trade mark is clearly shown on the surprisingly ornamental stand.

116 Harper, among whose trade marks was the word 'Beatrice', made gas irons of a different design from those of Cross. Harper was interested in export, as shown by the special packing.

117 The narrow tailor's iron shown here has been nick-named a 'weasel' because it can get into tight corners.

118 Three more tailor's irons on a cast stand not originally intended for that use.

119 Archibald Kenrick and Sons published a catalogue in about 1871 in which these 'specialist' irons were advertised. They were, one is assured, for dealing with all sorts of difficult situations. It has to be remembered that bonnets, mutton chop sleeves, laces, ribbons and bows were worn and would have to be ironed. Italian irons are commonly and incorrectly called gauffering irons. To gauffer is to crimp.

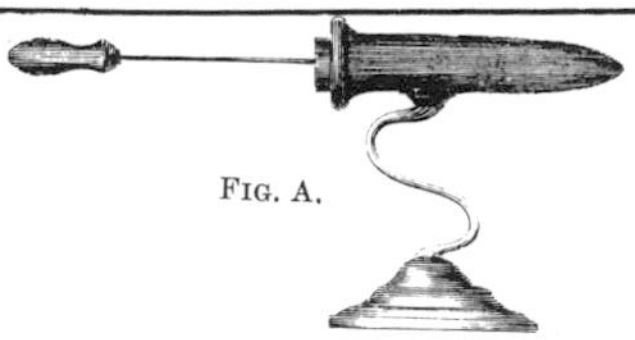

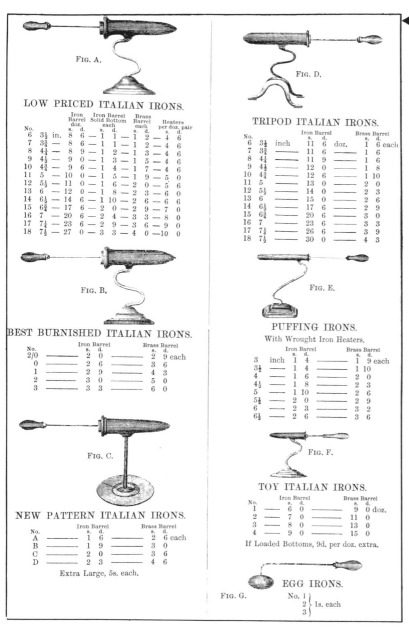

FIG. A.

LOW PRICED ITALIAN IRONS.

No.		Iron Barrel doz. s.	d.	Iron Barrel Solid Bottom each s.	d.	Brass Barrel each s.	d.	Heaters per doz. pair s.	d.
6	3½ in.	8	6	1	1	1	2	4	6
7	3¾ —	8	6	1	1	1	2	4	6
8	4¼ —	8	9	1	2	1	3	4	6
9	4½ —	9	0	1	3	1	5	4	6
10	4¾ —	9	6	1	4	1	7	4	6
11	5 —	10	0	1	5	1	9	5	0
12	5½ —	11	0	1	6	2	0	5	6
13	6 —	12	0	1	8	2	3	6	0
14	6½ —	14	6	1	10	2	6	6	6
15	6¾ —	17	6	2	0	2	9	7	0
16	7 —	20	6	2	4	3	3	8	0
17	7¼ —	23	6	2	9	3	6	9	0
18	7½ —	27	0	3	3	4	0	10	0

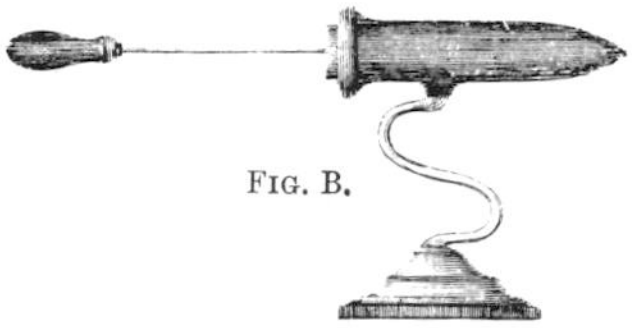

FIG. B.

BEST BURNISHED ITALIAN IRONS.

No.	Iron Barrel s.	d.	Brass Barrel s.	d.
2/0	2	0	2	9 each
0	2	6	3	6
1	2	9	4	3
2	3	0	5	0
3	3	3	6	0

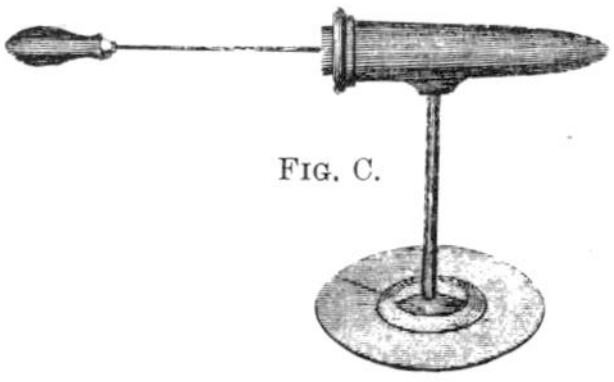

FIG. C.

NEW PATTERN ITALIAN IRONS.

No.	Iron Barrel s.	d.	Brass Barrel s.	d.
A	1	6	2	6 each
B	1	9	3	0
C	2	0	3	6
D	2	3	4	6

Extra Large, 5s. each.

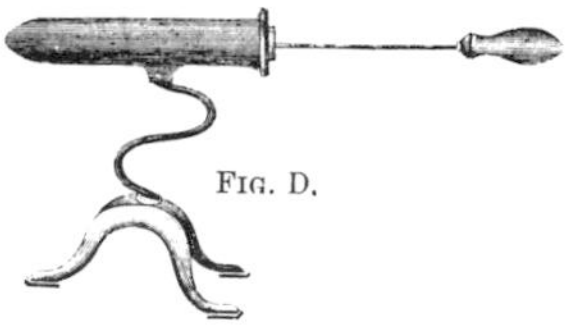

FIG. D.

TRIPOD ITALIAN IRONS.

No.		Iron Barrel s.	d.		Brass Barrel s.	d.
6	3½ inch	11	6	doz.	1	6 each
7	3¾	11	6		1	6
8	4¼	11	9		1	6
9	4½	12	0		1	8
10	4¾	12	6		1	10
11	5	13	0		2	0
12	5½	14	0		2	3
13	6	15	0		2	6
14	6½	17	6		2	9
15	6¾	20	6		3	0
16	7	23	6		3	3
17	7¼	26	6		3	9
18	7½	30	0		4	3

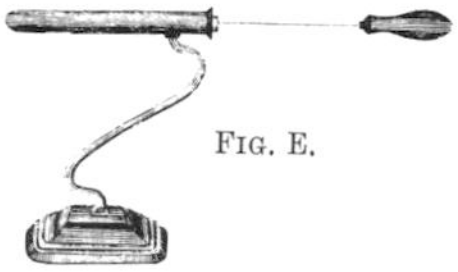

FIG. E.

PUFFING IRONS.

With Wrought Iron Heaters.

		Iron Barrel s.	d.	Brass Barrel s.	d.
3	inch	1	4	1	9 each
3½		1	4	1	10
4		1	6	2	0
4½		1	8	2	3
5		1	10	2	6
5½		2	0	2	9
6		2	3	3	2
6½		2	6	3	6

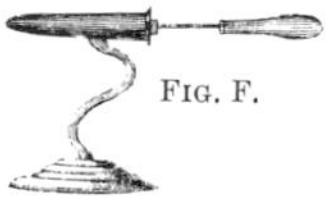

FIG. F.

TOY ITALIAN IRONS.

No.	Iron Barrel s.	d.	Brass Barrel s.	d.
1	6	0	9	0 doz.
2	7	0	11	0
3	8	0	13	0
4	9	0	15	0

If Loaded Bottoms, 9d. per doz. extra.

FIG. G.

EGG IRONS.

No. 1, 2, 3 — 1s. each

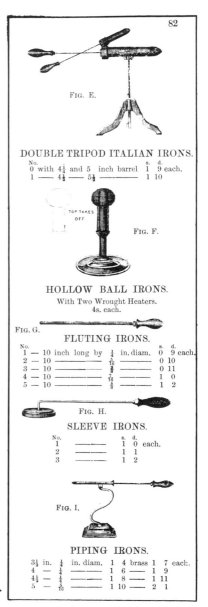

82

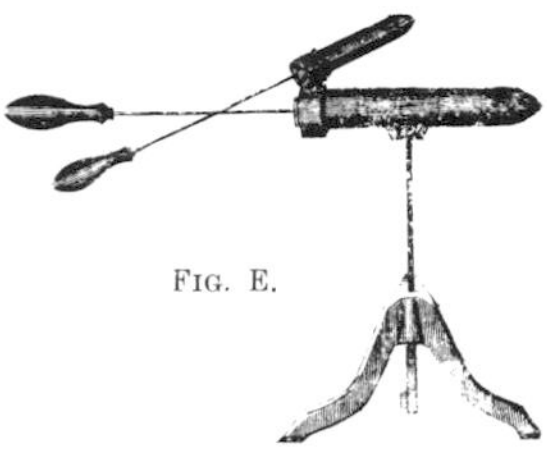

FIG. E.

DOUBLE TRIPOD ITALIAN IRONS.

No.		s.	d.
0	with 4¼ and 5 inch barrel	1	9 each.
1	— 4½ — 5½	1	10

FIG. F.

HOLLOW BALL IRONS.

With Two Wrought Heaters.
4s. each.

FIG. G.

FLUTING IRONS.

No.			s.	d.
1	10 inch long by	$\frac{1}{4}$ in. diam.	0	9 each.
2	10	$\frac{5}{16}$	0	10
3	10	$\frac{3}{8}$	0	11
4	10	$\frac{7}{16}$	1	0
5	10	$\frac{5}{8}$	1	2

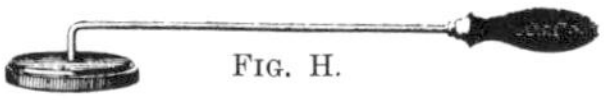

FIG. H.

SLEEVE IRONS.

No.	s.	d.
1	1	0 each.
2	1	1
3	1	2

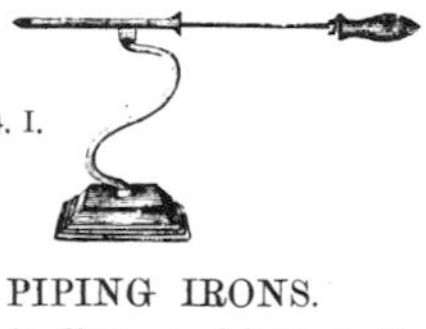

FIG. I.

PIPING IRONS.

3½ in.	$\frac{1}{4}$ in. diam.	1	4	brass 1	7 each.
4 —	$\frac{1}{4}$	1	6	1	9
4½ —	$\frac{1}{4}$	1	8	1	11
5 —	$\frac{5}{16}$	1	10	2	1

120 Another page from the same Kenrick catalogue. These irons were, it is said, invented in Italy at the time when many ruffles were the fashion.

121 As can be seen from these examples iron stands come in many, many patterns and are very collectable. William Cross catalogue.

▶

122 and 123 Collecting iron stands, or trivets as they are called in the USA and Canada, is a popular hobby particularly in North America. The majority of those illustrated are owned by Miss Pope.

▼

IRON STANDS

WITH IRON HANDLE.

No. 99.

Japanned and Polished Top.

No. 101.

Self Colour.
Japanned and Polished Top.

No. 102.

Self Colour.
Japanned and Polished Top.

WITH WOOD HANDLE.

No. 103.

Highly Polished Top.

No. 105.

Japanned Top and Polished on Edge.

No. 104.

Japanned and Polished Top.

No. 98.

Gilt Bronzed.

124-129 Those with the maker's name and/or initial are much sought after and at least one collector is trying to make a collection with initials from A to Z; a possibility because these everyday objects were made in thousands by hundreds of founders. As can be seen some were cast with holes for screws and they came in many sizes as indicated by the group of four hanging on the wall at Shelburne Museum. Pottstown, Pennsylvania was a foundry town.

130   A plain iron stand, cast in Montreal.

131   Two decorative iron stands. ▶

132 and 133   Two almost identical stands, one named 'The Royal' the other with no name.

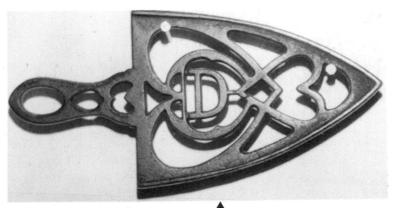

134 and 135　Two more iron stands with initials.

136　A damaged, but decorative stand.

137　Another stand made in Montreal.

5 At the Door and About the House

138   A knocker similar to No 255 in the Kenrick range, but not identified as such because no mark is visible.

So far we have dealt with cast iron used as decoration in architecture, cast iron used in the supply of heat and cast iron applied to methods of keeping clean and healthy. This chapter considers objects with less fundamental uses for the metal — uses to which other materials such as brass or wood could have been and were put to use, but where cast iron became predominent because it was strong, weather resistant and, above all, weighty. Thus it had a great appeal, for Victorian taste in all things tended to the belief that because a thing was solid and massy it was good, and certainly the items to be dealt with now were heavy. On the whole the articles which are found in this class can be described as assisting to make the mediocrity of life easier, more comfortable and more convenient and almost without exception they are most attractive to collectors. Their variety is enormous, each founder had his own ideas as to how they should be designed and although there was much copying among manufacturers there are subtle differences to be noted in a close study and this adds to the interest of a collection.

In this category among the most rewarding of items for the collector is Victorian door furniture. Door furniture in this context consists of knockers, knobs, letter slots, bell pulls and boot scrapers. Each household had to have its complement of each, for obvious reasons. The streets were unpaved and muddy, heavy doors needed a strong pull or push to move them and the electric door-bell with which the caller can now draw attention to his presence had not yet made its appearance. Then when Rowland Hill introduced the penny post in 1840, the sending and receiving of letters became much more frequent, so with as many as four deliveries a day the letter slot, sometimes combined with the knocker, became not only necessary but fashionable. In those days the postman always knocked twice to announce the arrival of mail. With the possible exception of boot scrapers all these items were also made in brass, but cast iron seems to have had not only the appeal noted above but had the added advantage of being cheaper while it did not need the daily application of polish. It is thought that they all made their appearance — except for letter slots — in the very early years of the nineteenth century. There is some evidence to this effect in the fact that Kenrick's catalogue of 1834 advertised them all and Kenrick was certainly not the only maker — Coalbrookdale and others including Falkirk all had their products for the household doorway. Designers were influenced by

Egyptian, Chinese, Japanese or Continental motifs depending on what particular fashion was prevalent at the time.

Door knockers, knobs and bell pulls were of one basic pattern and so there is little to be said of them in relation to this, but of the boot scraper this is not true. The boot scraper came in four different varieties. First there was the scraper set into the stone or brick wall of the house. These were far from popular because they were so difficult to use but the variation which was set firmly into the stone of the step was a better design and could not be stolen except with difficulty. They were as permanent as the steps into which they were set as was the scraper moulded with the railings leading to the door of the house (Fig 8). Many of this type have disappeared with the demolition of elderly premises, in the same way that the railings themselves have suffered. Finally there is the pan scraper, often a much more attractive article which was portable and was made in very ornate designs. As the name implies it is a pan to catch mud, supporting the scraper which was cast as an integral part of the whole or cast separately and bolted together later. Sometimes they were combined with side brushes. So popular are pan scrapers as collectors' items that it is necessary to use catalogue illustrations to show the wide variety offered for sale at one time, and they are so practical that reproductions in cast iron are now available.

Inside the door was another array of cast iron art, for here one could find hat, coat and umbrella stands. As can be seen they are of the greatest interest to the collector because of their beauty, variety and also their utility. Perhaps this cannot be completely true of the enormous coat and hat stands of the time but a cast iron umbrella stand is a treasure to anyone who has had the pleasure of owning one. Tucked away in the entrance hall it will not only excite favourable comment, it will collect to itself all sorts of long thin unwieldy objects that may be required only occasionally but are most conveniently kept near the door. They are useful and decorative, valuable collectors' pieces and memorials to a more gracious age. No hallway should be without one.

Still another item of door furniture to have commanded attention over the years from collectors of cast iron is the door stop, more correctly called the porter for it was in fact a true attendant at a door or gate, just as the dictionary states. The common, and possibly even true, story behind the evolution of porters concerns an invention designed to deal with a common and most irritating habit to which some persons are prone: leaving doors open. It is said that in 1775 John Izon and Thomas Whitehurst overcame the problem when they patented their 'rising hinge with steel roller' which caused any door so equipped slowly and automatically to close. Whatever the truth of this tale the rising hinge did create a new situation — how to keep it from operating when it was necessary or desirable for the door to stay open? Perhaps a wedge, a stone or a piece of furniture could have offered a solution, albeit one lacking elegance but soon both the iron and brass founders provided a much better answer — door porters. During the house

139 Possibly Kenrick's No 405 of about 1880, but if so the base has been broken as it is usually circular. The cast iron letter slot is quite ornate. No maker known.

141 This could possibly be the Wellington knocker made by Kenrick and shown in their catalogue for 1840.

142 Although similar to pattern 423 of 1880 from Kenrick, it may not have been made by them as founders copied each other.

143 Pattern No 224 from the Kenrick 1871 catalogue is much like this.

140 Kenrick's name appears on the back on this combined letter slot and knocker. It appeared first in their 1880 catalogue as pattern No 422. A lozenge on the back shows the design was registered in that year. See also Fig 373.

building boom of the nineteenth century they were cast by the thousands and, in iron, they sold for 2s 6d to 7s (12.5p to 35p, about 25c to 70c) each. They were offered in at least three different finishes, the cheapest being japanned black, with the more durable Berlin Black commanding a substantial premium. They could also be obtained with a bronze finish to resemble the more expensive metal.

Possibly Archibald Kenrick and Sons of West Bromwich were the most prolific manufacturers for they illustrated forty-eight styles in 1871 and forty-nine in 1880. Coalbrookdale, too, had a substantial number of models in their range; thirty-six in 1875. Other ironfounders such as Falkirk, the Welsh iron masters at Blaenavon and Aberavon; T. J. Jones, Pentyrch; Harper & Com-

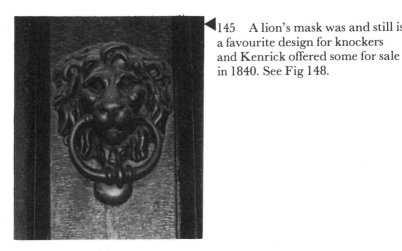

145 A lion's mask was and still is a favourite design for knockers and Kenrick offered some for sale in 1840. See Fig 148.

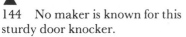

144 No maker is known for this sturdy door knocker.

146 This shape is mostly seen in brass — and it looks very well if kept polished. This is in iron.

147 Another design of lion's mask knocker. Maker unknown.

pany; Baldwin, Son & Company, and Bowling Iron Works of Bradford, Yorkshire all sold cast iron porters at the height of their popularity which, judging from the Kenrick catalogues, appears to have been roughly from about 1850 to 1880. In fact possibly most iron foundries tried their hands — some say as a means of keeping their employees busy during bad times — at producing door porters. Unhappily only a few were proud enough of their work to put a trade mark on their products, so that identification of makers other than those most active in the trade is seldom possible and porters with a Coalbrookdale, Falkirk or Kenrick mark are most valuable.

Designing door porters may have been a specialised art in the same way that designers of postage stamps can be said to require particular abilities, but who these artists were or where they came from is still unknown. Looking at a selection of their work one cannot help being impressed by the catholicity of their tastes since here are to be found intermingled, abstract, allegorical and realistic representations. One doubts whether they were created

148 A copy of a page from the catalogue published in 1871 by Kenrick showing their range at that time. Most were being made in 1840, but No 311 did not appear until 1871.

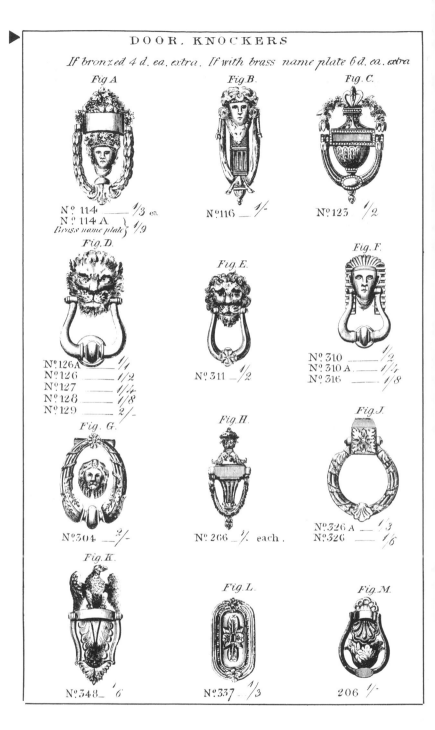

DOOR. KNOCKERS

If bronzed 4 d. ea. extra. If with brass name plate 6 d. ea. extra

by only one craftsman for on a single page of the Kenrick catalogue there are illustrated sixteen of the forty-eight sold at that time; they include not only a fox head, but a bowl of fruit which may be contrasted with the ten abstracts, an Egyptian motif, and even Aesop's fable of the thirsty stork depicted. It is a known fact, of course, that founders with aspirations in the artistic iron field

No 20. 5 inch. No 21. 5 inch. No 22. 5 inch.

149 Baldwin, Son & Company made a variety of castings to be used with door-bells. Pulls, fancy and plain, sunk and raised and some with legends such as 'House', 'Visitors' or 'Servants'.

GENERAL IRONMONGERY.

GOTHIC HANDLES.

JAPANNED.

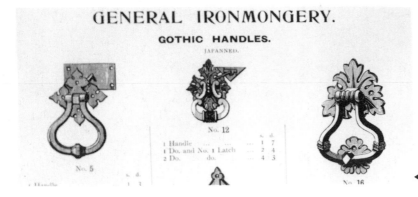

150 Baldwin's 1898 catalogue at a time when enthusiasm for Gothic taste in literature and art was high.

employed designers of great skill, some of whom came from as far afield as Continental Europe. On the other hand there was a good deal of copying or 'pirating' so one finds Coalbrookdale, Falkirk and Kenrick with very similar swans, for example, while Coalbrookdale's very popular knight in armour in a Gothic arch was much imitated and counterparts of Kenrick's Highland soldier have been found in other catalogues and were made by countless unnamed manufacturers. Other examples could be mentioned and bearing in mind that there does not seem to have been much attempt to register designs with the Patent Office the numerous instances of similitude are not surprising.

So avid are collectors of door porters to expand their collections that prices have risen dramatically in the recent past. At one time it would have been possible to purchase a good lion for as little as £2.50 ($5) but now it could command as much as £25 and so rare are some examples of this type of article that they could not be bought at any price. In fact door porters seem largely to have disappeared from the market or are snapped up too quickly for them to remain on a dealer's shelves for very long. As a result modern reproductions of old designs are available and can be impossible to detect if the old patterns have been used. A large but far from exhaustive selection of illustrations has been included to give the reader a better idea of the extent of this particular corner of the collector's world.

Once past the front door and through the entrance hall there was some further use of iron in the living quarters of a home of the 1850s. Aside from fireplaces, dealt with in another chapter, there was for a while a vogue for furniture constructed in part or wholly of cast iron — tables, chairs, beds and benches. These are described in Chapter 7, Iron for Everything. Fashion changed and

151 Pan boot scrapers like this good example command high prices as they are now rather scarce.

152 Less well preserved but still in use, this pan scraper has no mark.

153 Pan scrapers were offered by Archibald Kenrick. Some of the motifs used for door porters were adapted for use as supports for scrapers.

608 — 4/8 each.

609 4/4

610 — 2 3

613 With Brushes. 8/.
Without Brushes. 6/.

611 2 3

614 With Brushes. 10/.
Without Brushes. 7 6

612 3 6

615 — 5/9

154 As these scrapers were not fixed they could easily be removed and lost. This is interesting for its triple blade and open base.

wood, which had always been the preferred material for such items, soon returned to favour but there was one area, the kitchen, where iron reigned with such authority that it has only recently been deposed. In the Victorian kitchen cast iron was as vital as coal for fuel, for from it was constructed the ranges on which cooking was carried out and a multitude of pots, pans, slicers, grinders, shellers, beaters, squeezers and peelers to take some of the drudgery out of food preparation. In fact mechanisation in the

155 From an old, unidentified catalogue comes this quartet of umbrella stands. The activities pictured are Woodman, Piscator, Hunter and Fruit gatherer.

156 From the same catalogue. These stands, on the other hand, seem to have a less traditionally romantic origin for their design, and lean more towards the Gothic in origin.

kitchen started well over 100 years ago when the iron industry provided gadgets to make more efficient use of human muscle power. To a large extent cast iron had, because of its lower price, replaced brass and copper for pots and pans by the middle of the nineteenth century although it had begun to do so almost at the beginning of the eighteenth when Abraham Darby developed his method of casting three-legged cauldrons at Coalbrookdale. At that time most items of this description were imported from Europe and were so valuable they were often mentioned in house-

157 Umbrella or stick stand in use. These command high prices whereas a few years ago they were given away as junk.

158 Corner stands like this are most unusual. Painted black with the leafy design in gold it is a handsome piece.

159 An umbrella stand that would grace the hall of a big house in the Hunting Shires. Unfortunately there is no indication as to where it was cast and which artist made the pattern.

160 The portrait of the young
Queen Victoria, in a rather severe
mood, cast with the rest and then
painted makes this an interesting
stand.

161 As Castle Museum, York,
dressed a Regency set-piece they
added an umbrella stand of the
period and included suitable
umbrellas and parasols.

162 A rather ecclesiastical stand,
suitable for a Church porch, with
a large capacity to gather a flock
of umbrellas from the congrega-
tion on a rainy day.

163   Just three of the many coat, hat and umbrella stands made by the Coalbrookdale Company and shown in their catalogue of 1875. The left-hand stand is 7ft 4in high and projects 14in from the wall. The width was 3ft 6in and the weight enormous. The two largest had brass hat rails and mirrors. These items are now very scarce and these catalogue illustrations are valuable evidence that they were actually available.

hold inventories particularly in wills, and clearly Darby had his eye on this trade. From its inception and for a long period afterwards a major portion of the Dale Company's business was in these pots, made in various sizes ranging up to several feet in diameter. In a lighter vein the latter were often depicted as very popular in less civilized parts of the world for boiling European missionaries and explorers. In the English household on the other hand a pot was of use not only for boiling, for it could be made into a primitive oven by providing it with a cover. Thus when the fire was heaped over an upright pot the bread baked therein was said to be 'pot-oven' bread, but if it was baked in an inverted pot then it was called 'up-set' bread.

Three-legged pots or those with bail handles, were entirely satisfactory cooking utensils for as long as the large open wood fireplace with its crane from which the latter could be hung was in use, but as fireplaces were modified they became less acceptable. Now the need was for a flat bottomed device which could stand on the hob and because of its shape give better transfer of heat to the contents. Thus pots, kettles and pans became standardised to the shape we know today. The illustrations also show that the house-wife of the past had a pan for just about every one of her kitchen

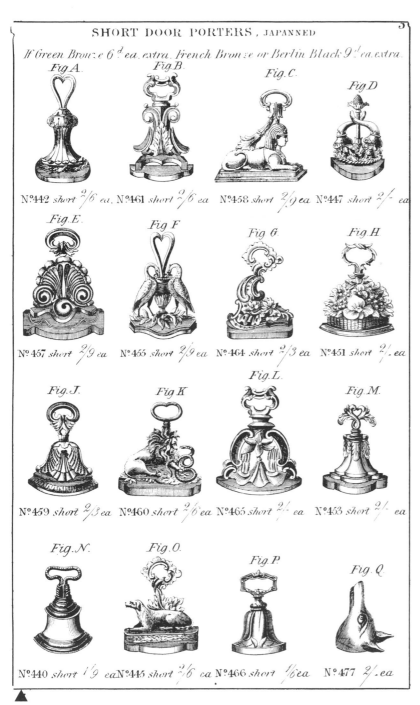

SHORT DOOR PORTERS, JAPANNED

If Green Bronze 6ᵈ ea. extra. French Bronze or Berlin Black 9ᵈ ea. extra.

Fig. A.   Fig. B.   Fig. C.   Fig D

Nº 442 *short* 2/6 *ea.*   Nº 461 *short* 2/6 *ea*   Nº 458 *short* 2/9 *ea*   Nº 447 *short* 2/- *ea*

Fig. E.   Fig F   Fig G.   Fig. H.

Nº 457 *short* 2/9 *ea*   Nº 455 *short* 2/9 *ea*   Nº 464 *short* 2/3 *ea*   Nº 451 *short* 2/- *ea*

Fig. J.   Fig K   Fig. L.   Fig. M.

Nº 459 *short* 2/3 *ea*   Nº 460 *short* 2/6 *ea*   Nº 465 *short* 2/- *ea*   Nº 453 *short* 2/- *ea*

Fig. N.   Fig. O.   Fig. P.   Fig. Q.

Nº 440 *short* 1/9 *ea*   Nº 445 *short* 2/6 *ea*   Nº 466 *short* 1/6 *ea*   Nº 477 2/- *ea*

165   This door porter uses the same theme. It is very solid and about 11in high. Made by William James at Pentyrch Ironworks, Wales, between 1860 and 1875.

164   A page from Kenrick's catalogue of 1871. There are also thirty-two other door porters in the same catalogue. Notice the adaptation of Aesop's fable where two cranes or storks are dropping pebbles into a vase until water rises sufficiently for them to drink.

166   These long handled dog porters often have had the handle broken off although some were cast with a short handle. This is about 16in high.

167 So many statues of the Duke of Wellington were cast that porters of this design are far from rare. The 'Iron Duke' must have held many a door open in his time.

tasks. And of course there were in those days many more chores with which she had to contend. She might have to make her own preserves or let her milk settle to skim off the cream, she most certainly would have bigger joints of meat to roast; the electric kettle had yet to be invented so she would boil water on the stove, and the non-stick frying pan was a long way in the future. Lighter aluminium or stainless steel ware has long been in vogue but it can be said of cast iron cooking equipment that although it was heavy heat distribution was more even, scorching less of a problem, and this perhaps explains a recent return to traditional cast iron.

As the desire for an easier life became stronger and as iron-founders sought new outlets for their metal and expertise a tidal wave of invention gained momentum, inundating the kitchen with gadgets. The maize grinder replaced mortar and pestle, beans could be cut, fruit sliced, marmalade prepared, coffee ground, food weighed, chopped or minced. The pressure cooker, first introduced in 1680 as 'Papin's Digester', could now be manufactured and sold at a reasonable price, making its use economically feasible for the smaller families. There were even domestic sausage machines, apple peelers and corers (Goodell's patent of 1863), lemon squeezers and a very useful labour saving device before there were stainless steel knives — a burnishing machine to eliminate the task of rubbing them with a cork or a cloth to which Bath brick had been applied. Many of these inventions, sad to say, have not survived; who now uses maize grinders or coffee mills? — and one is unlikely to discover a household with a fruit slicer, but others, left by the receding wave of cast iron invention have proved so durable as to find continued employment in many kitchens still. As they reach the end of their long and useful life, however, they are being replaced with modern, less cumbersome and lighter articles to which very often electric power has been added, but instead of being thrown on the scrap heap as in the past they are now sought after by collectors.

168 A very fine casting of a dog with the head turned to form a handle when this porter was to be moved. There is a lozenge on the back, see Fig 375. Much imitated by founders; 14½ in high. Originally at the Gulbenkian Museum of Oriental Art, this and many other pieces of collectable cast iron are now on display at the North of England Open Air Museum, Beamish, County Durham.

169   A popular Coalbrookdale porter was the knight in full armour standing in a Gothic arch. It was copied by most of the iron-founders in Britain.

170   Another warrior with a patriotic message on the base, 'Bonnie Scotland'.

171   Admiral Nelson after he had lost his arm at an attack on Santa Cruz de Tenerife, 1797. This stop is painted in authentic colours and 24 in high.

172   Britannia at sea on her wooden-walled war ship with its flag, her shield and a lion by her side. 17 in high.

173   A Scotish soldier about 14 in high. It may be one of a pair as his weapon is in the left hand. These porters are often seen with the top of the axe broken off.

73

174　The uniform is thought to be similar to that used in the Crimean war and the base may possibly depict the famous charge of the Light Brigade at the battle of Balaclava, October 25 1854.

175　On the base of this porter are the words 'Britain's Pride' and it is one of many similar porters praising the Navy.

176　'Jaques' on the back of this porter indicates that it is a representation of the character in Shakespeare's play *As You Like It*, who speaks the well-known lines 'and all the world's a stage and all the men and women merely players. . . .' The design was registered 1 November 1853.

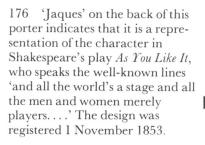

177 and 178　Punch and his wife Judy. Pair of porters representing popular English puppets, modelled after the cover picture for *Punch* a humorous magazine started in 1844. The cover was designed by Richard Doyle, an Anglo-Irish painter and illustrator. Punch is a quarrelsome joker who beats his wife, escapes arrest by thumping the policeman and even hangs his hangman.

179   Tom Matthews, a clown who was successor to Joe Grimaldi the first 'modern' type of clown. Matthews, who died in 1850, had a catch phrase 'Don't You Tell'.

180   Bacchus, Greek god of wine with his cap conveniently shaped as a handle. Painted in bright colours.

181   Another character from Greek mythology. The infant Hercules, later famous for his twelve 'Labours', but here shown struggling with serpents put in his bed by his father's jealous wife.

182   The goddess Medusa, queen of the Gorgons of Greek Mythology. To look upon her face and hair, a crown of serpents, was to be turned to stone. A Falkirk design registered 20 July 1872.

183   The original iron pattern from which the sand mould was made for Kenrick's porter No 459.

184   Although quite common these lions are much sought after. It is over 15 in high and weighs more than 10 lb.

185   Door porter marked W on the reverse and 15 in high.

186   An uncommon porter illustrating a bear stealing honey from a bee hive.

187   Rebecca at the well. The name means 'Tie or Bind Fast' and she was chosen, because of her kindness, to be the wife of Isaac and was mother of Jacob and Esau. (Genesis 24-31.)

188   A door porter of a young gallant and his lady.

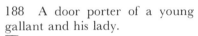

189   Military figures were popular as door porters.

190   War-like angels are not often encountered. This may be a door stop or it may be an ornament since the feet make it unsuitable as a porter.

191 From the Kenrick collection this 9in high porter is pattern No 488. The brass handle is bolted to the cast iron base.

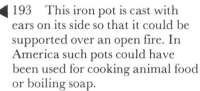

192 Cast in an unknown Welsh foundry in the nineteenth century this porter is part of the collection at the Welsh Folk Museum.

193 This iron pot is cast with ears on its side so that it could be supported over an open fire. In America such pots could have been used for cooking animal food or boiling soap.

194 Pots manufactured by Baldwin, Son and Company.

UPRIGHT OVAL POTS,
With Saucepans of one pint each, fitted into the covers.

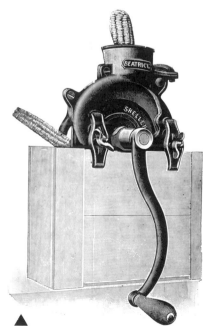

195 This well-worn 'Gipsy' kettle is marked J. & J. Siddons, West Bromwich. Manufacturers called them 'tea kitchens' and they were made to be suspended over an open fire. The long spout made it possible to draw off the contents without being burned.

196 From John Harper's catalogue comes this maize sheller, just one of many models by them, for use in farms and homes up until the middle of this century. The catalogue is dated 1932.

BELLIED COFFEE POTS,

New Pattern.

COFFEE POTS.

UPRIGHT COFFEE POTS,

197 These iron pots made by Baldwin, Son & Company make excellent collector's pieces, but they are scarce.

GROCERS' MILL, WITH WHEEL.

No.						s.	d.	
3	...	...	...	...	...	8	0	each.
4	...	...	...	...	...	10	0	,,
5	...	...	...	...	...	12	0	,,
6	...	...	...	...	.	14	0	,,
7	...	...	...	...	...	17	0	,,
8	...	...	...	...	...	20	0	,,
9	...	...	...	...	...	25	0	,,

ROUND BOX COFFEE MILL.

			If Brass Hoppers.		
No.	s.	d.		s.	d.
10	...	3 0	...	3	6 each.
11	...	3 3	...	4	0 ,,
12	...	3 8	...	4	6 ,,
13	...	4 0	...	5	0 ,,

OPEN.   CLOSED.

PORTABLE COFFEE MILL.
3s. 6d. each.

198 Some of these coffee mills are still in use but the number is declining rapidly. Many homes would have had one and they were once a feature of many shops where the smell of freshly ground coffee created a most pleasant atmosphere.

199 A four-legged pot only about 5in in diameter. It was intended to rest among the flames.

200 A coffee mill in wood and iron with a drawer under.

201 Coffee grinder for a grocery store made in Philadelphia, USA.

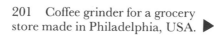

79

202 Davidson's Coffee Roaster patented July 1886.

203 Apples were very important foodstuffs in northern America and Canada. They were dried in the sun for use in the winter and thus much ingenuity was exerted in finding quicker ways of peeling, slicing and coring the fruit. This complicated machine called the 'Bonanza' cored and peeled apples in one operation. Made by Goddel Company.

204 An apple peeler showing the knife and prongs on which the apple was placed.

205 The apple is plastic but serves to show how a simple peeler would operate.

▲ 206 Here the blade that peeled the apple can be seen at the right centre.

▲ 207 Once the apple had been peeled and cored it was sliced and this is a machine for making seven slices at once. The final dried product was called an apple ring. Shelburne Museum has a large collection of peelers.

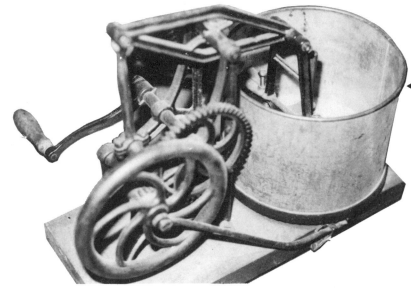

◀ 208 This complicated looking machine is possibly a potato masher.

209 A good solid cast iron kitchen scale with cast iron weights still in use. Although marked as made in West Bromwich the ◀ maker is unknown.

210 Why John Harper's
'Beatrice' fruit slicer was for export only is an unsolved mystery.
Marmalade machines were as
common in the past as food blend-
ers are now.

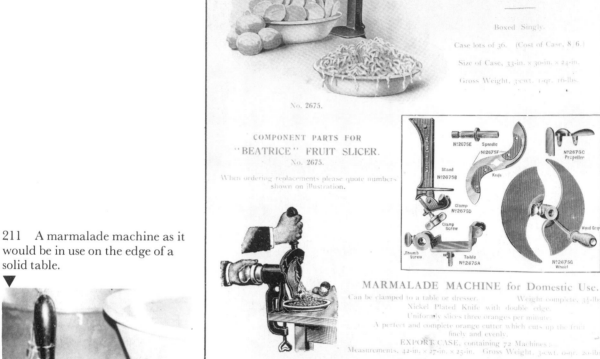

211 A marmalade machine as it
would be in use on the edge of a
solid table.

212 Knife cleaners or burnishers
were for use in large houses or
hotels. This was made in Birmingham and is marked 'Kent's
patent'. Knives were pushed into
slots around the perimeter of the
drum and the handle turned.

213 Left is a cast iron griddle and right a muffin dish. Both these are of Canadian manufacture and collectable. The centre item is an instrument for breaking lumps of ice. A spring handle kept the hands from getting cold.

214 Another Canadian muffin dish.

215 Cast iron mortar and pestle. ▶

216 A modern waffle iron made by Bofors in Sweden.
▼

GRIP BROILER AND TOASTER.

As shown—9 in. size, 2 3; 10 in. size, 2 6.
If without Perforations for Pancakes, etc.—
9 in. size, 2/-; 10 in. size, 2/3.

WAFFLE IRON.

For Baking Batter Cakes or Waffles on a Stove or Range.

PRICE   5

217 Scottish waffle iron and toaster from the Smith and Well-stood range.

6 Miniature Grates and Mantel Ornaments

218 About 12in high, this little grate has brass fire bars adding greatly to its value and appearance. These would have been placed in the mould before the molten metal was poured. The coat of arms may be that of William IV but corrosion makes it impossible to be certain.

219 Although the oak leaves and acorns are very much the same as those in the previous illustration we find a very different surround and fireback for the grate. Here stylized roses, clover leaf and honeysuckle are used. The portrait heads might be William IV although the arms seem to be those of Victoria. There is a portion broken from the top of the coat of arms.

Those items of collectable cast iron described in the previous chapters have all had some useful purpose although many, such as balcony railings, boot scrapers and door furniture have also been given considerable style and beauty by those artists who designed for the foundries in which their manufacture took place. They were intended to make living more comfortable, lighter, cleaner, warmer and some even assisted in an improvement in the standard of cooking. These objects have become collectable mainly because of their place in social history and only to a lesser extent because of their artistic appeal. There are, however, large numbers of the products of the foundry trade where no utilitarian purpose can be discerned, where little aesthetic value is evident and where the quality of workmanship is often not of the best and yet it is these unrefined, sometimes ugly, frequently badly made pieces that have perhaps the greatest appeal to collectors. This group of useless objects falls conveniently into two distinct classes — miniature or model grates and mantelshelf ornaments — with the second category capable of being subdivided still further. Thousands were manufactured between about 1850 and 1910, but by whom we are not sure, as there is little evidence. So far none have been found in old catalogues nor do many have an identifying mark either in the form of the maker's name or the registration number.

The origins and *raison d'etre* of the first class of these mysterious objects — miniature grates — remains obscure, at least to the author, who is unconvinced of the validity of theories put forward by some experts, for it seems that each is based only on supposition and the facts have yet to be established. Five different reasons for their existence have been advanced and argued with a greater or lesser degree of emotion dependent on how far its protagonist is committed. One authority on iron has advanced his opinion that smaller miniature grates (and the author has seen one of this type) were used as mantel ornaments and the larger kind as door porters. Latterly they have found employment as porters certainly but the protruding feet possessed by most of them tend to stick under the door making them difficult to remove. Some, too, have rough backs likely to scratch the polished or painted surface of the door while others have loose, decorative brass curbs, both obvious disadvantages when employed as porters. A second suggestion is that they were made for dolls' houses but this seems unlikely as their size, often 10-15in high would make them unsuitable for any

220 A pair of grates about 12in high, one of which has been repaired. That on the left has an undamaged pot-crane. Both have a mixture of religious symbols and tools of the mason's or ironfounder's trades. Said by one authority to be Masonic.

but the most imposing of dolls' mansions. There are also those who subscribe to the belief that a miniature fire-grate was made as an 'apprentice piece'; that is an object prepared to show the degree of skill achieved after a young man's training had been completed, but many of the castings are so crude it is highly unlikely that they would have been looked upon with any pride and in any case the large numbers surviving seem to indicate that they were manufactured in quantity.

The favourite and most often quoted suggested reason for the existence of model grates is that they were salesmen's samples. Those who advance this theory cite the fact that in the past representatives called on customers using horse and cart or buggy as a conveyance and they believe that a representative for an ironfounder carried miniature samples rather than the real article. There are a large number of vocal advocates of the explanation, but one wonders why a salesman needed to carry samples at all when ironfounders published such well illustrated and voluminous catalogues which they gave to their representatives and also sent to their prospective customers. One wonders, too, what the reactions of the purchaser of a grate would be when on delivery he saw that it had been shorn of all the surrounding decoration of oak or other leaves, coats of arms and other ornaments present on the miniature. Lastly there is a possibility that ironfounders provided these ornate miniatures as advertisements. Just as butchers used to have miniature beasts in their windows, or fishmongers displayed their wares in the same way so it is possible ironmongers would put a model grate or two in the window or on the counter to indicate they were ready to supply their customers from stock. No logical objections have been raised so far against this suggestion, but neither is there

221 Although the oak leaf and acorn motif is retained the rest of the grate is entirely changed both in shape of hob and in ornamentation.

222   This grate is different again and although it still has its oak leaves and acorns the rest is of a much simpler design. Two thistles, one on top of each column, may indicate Scottish origins.

223   Because of the heavy top this grate is 14in high and, like most of the others, 12in wide. Why the dog or lion is seated above the fire cannot easily be explained nor is it possible to give a reason why the pattern maker did not carve a mirror image for the oak leaf design and thus get a symmetrical casting pattern.

224   Acanthus leaves have replaced the oak and acorn motif at the sides of this model grate. They make a more symmetrical pattern. The coat of arms looks like that of Queen Victoria but is supported by a rather confusing collection of loops and curliques. The brass fender is probably not original.

225 Even a close examination of the four female figures does not reveal the story they may be relating. On one hand they may be the four seasons or, on the other, it is possibly the story of Eve being tempted by the Serpent in the Garden of Eden.

226 The collection of motifs makes this grate something special. The female figures are similar to those in the previous illustration; Phoenix rising from the flames and disappearing up the chimney is unusual and we also have Napoleon crossing the

Alps. See also Fig 232 where the same motif is used. Napoleon, a historical figure of some renown, was not often used by artists in cast iron as a model. The same motif has been seen as a design at the base of street lamp posts.

any supporting evidence in its favour. Until someone can say from personal experience which of these explanations is correct, the mystery is likely to remain unsolved.

As will be evident from the illustrations most model grates were of the hob type popular in the nineteenth century and designed to fit into the place formerly occupied by the wood fire, but with wide variations in minor details and ornamentation, and the reason for the latter is almost as great a subject for speculation as that of their origin. For instance Fig 220 shows a pair of grates, one of which has been broken, on which the ornamentation could be of tools of the moulder's trade or alternatively of some secret society but there does seem to be a religious motif with what might be a crude reconstruction of the Resurrection above the fire place. Following this pair are grates featuring supporting oak leaves and acorn ornamentation of a very similar kind but the design of the surrounds, fire backs and coats of arms of all differ widely. Loose brass fire bars grace the front of Fig 218 and add to its attractive appearance and surmounting it may be the coat of arms of William IV although it is difficult to tell because the casting is so rough. At the same time the heads on either side of the arms on Fig 219 could be portraits of this monarch although here the arms appear to be those of Victoria. This grate, a nice sharp casting, also incorporates in the surround and fireback clover leaf, rose and

227 Another unusual design for a miniature grate with only a few of the traditional motifs such as the honeysuckle. It has a peculiar form of fire bars in brass.

228 Although only part of this grate is of cast iron, the rest being of steel, it is included because it is very different from all the rest.

stylized honeysuckle devices often found in a modified form in castings for other purposes such as railings and gates. A distinguishing feature of the next grates illustrated (Figs 221-3) is the lazy attitude of the lion and unicorn supporters to the coats of arms. They are in a position of lassitude similar to those in the coats of arms on the frontispiece to Kenrick's catalogue of 1836 yet they have differences which cannot always be accounted for by the quality of the casting.

In Fig 224 there is shown a grate with acanthus leaves at each side, replacing the oak leaf and acorn motif so often used. This grate also has a very different coat of arms, and the surround and the fireback could have come from the same mould as the grate in Fig 219 although, in fact, acanthus leaves, arms and grate were all cast together; only the fireback and base were attached later. The brass hob or fender may not have been original equipment. Examination of figures 225-6 will show puzzling similarities and differences to which no easy explanation will be found. For example who or what are the female figures used as supporters — are they the four seasons or do they represent Eve in the Garden of Eden being tempted by the Serpent — the castings are too rough to allow positive identification. Although it is possible to understand why the fire back portrays Phoenix rising from the flames it is difficult to see what connection the unlikely picture of Napoleon crossing the Alps on a horse has with firegrates. The whole subject of model grates is a field in which further and more detailed investigation could bring much interest to collectors for there are a large number of questions still to be answered.

229 It must be presumed from the motif of thistles that this grate was made for Scotland or was made there. It is one of the best and sharpest castings in the series although the base has been replaced. The whole is highly polished and shines like silver.

In the first paragraph of this chapter there is the comment that there are two categories of purely decorative and very collectable castings and we now deal with the second — mantelshelf ornaments. They, like model grates, give rise to the question — why were they made, and although the suggested answer may not satisfy entirely there is some evidence that they could have been the modern replacement for pagan household gods. In ancient days each dwelling had an image to which the inhabitants paid tribute — the Romans worshipped their lares, figures of young people dressed in short tunics holding in one hand a drinking horn and in the other a cup. They had Vesta, goddess of the hearth with whom might be found Juno, Minerva and others enshrined as protectors of individual homes. Egyptians, too, set up images of their gods and worshipped them daily to ward off evil and bring good luck to the houses in which they were worshipped. Christianity forbade such practices and frowned on idolatry but the desire to have some household god, not so much as an object of worship, more to bring good luck appears to be firmly fixed in the human, and for example horse shoes are still hung over doors and fireplaces and medals are still kept as talismans. The superstition of humankind, and the need for protection against bad luck, could go a long way towards explaining the existence of Staffordshire pottery figures and the brass or iron mantelshelf ornaments manufactured all through Victoria's reign and into the 1920s. That they were still in demand at that late date is indicated by a catalogue of 1922 advertising thirty-six models of mantel ornaments in brass. They ranged through horses to seated women named after the continents of Asia, Africa, America and Europe. Although the castings appear, from the catalogue illustrations to be crude, Pearson-Page of Birmingham, now no longer in existence, had, it seems a thriving trade in this kind of product. It is possible that iron-founders were still making their versions of similar items only 50 or 60 years ago but the author unfortunately has no evidence one way or the other, since he has not found any catalogues offering them for sale.

Although this explanation of the growth of an industry making images may be disputed there will be no doubt that collecting mantelshelf ornaments can be as fascinating a hobby as is that of acquiring Staffordshire pottery figures, a very well documented area of the collector's world. Like the latter, the former are often portraits of famous, popular or even criminal personages of their era, many of whom have lost their identity through the passage of time. Sometimes therefore a good deal of research is required to rediscover the name of the person or the event being commemorated. This adds greatly to the fun of collecting and gives very great satisfaction when a search has been successful. As has been noted above these ornaments fall into several categories because the artists who made the designs drew their inspiration from various sources. Portraits of people, characters from literature or fable, historic events and idealised subjects such as animals, form the main types. Research into the past history of some of the

230   The story of 'Blind Jack' born John Metcalfe of Knaresborough (1717-1810) is an astonishing one. He became blind at six years of age but learned to play the fiddle, ride, swim, build houses, bridges and is famous for the many roads constructed by him. About 8in high.

231   This portrait bust of the 'Iron Duke' of Wellington shows the famous nose and the casting is marked Crowley & Co, Manchester. 9½in high.

232 A chimney ornament portrait of Napoleon crossing the Alps on a horse. It is said to be after a painting by Atelier de Jacques-Louis David entitled 'Crossing the Alps'. Although this artist painted five using the same theme, none is in England. Another version by de Laroche hangs in the main stair well of the Walker Art Gallery, Liverpool.

233 General Charles George (Chinese) Gordon (1833-85) born at Woolwich, son of General H. W. Gordon, Royal Artillery, he died at Khartoum 26 January 1885. General Garnet Joseph Wolseley (1833-1913) was sent to relieve Gordon and was only a few hours too late. Among his many other exploits he commanded an expedition which marched 2,000 miles across north-west Canada to put down the Louis Riel rebellion in 1870.

234 'Dr Jim' was Sir Leander Starr Jameson (1853-1917) who, in December 1895, lead a raid into the Transvaal, Southern Africa and who has been said to have been the direct cause of the Boer War of 1899-1902.

235 Reverend Joshua Brooks, a principal character in the Victorian book *The Manchester Man*. The story of how his identity was discovered is given in the text.

subjects used for mantelshelf ornaments can be assisted greatly by the use of old newspapers or magazines, but sometimes luck can play a great part in finding the name of some obscure person. Sometimes, too, bad fortune for someone else can mean a clue for the searcher as in the case of the fat little man with a flat hat and a book under his arm (Fig 235). This badly corroded effigy is one of many brought to auction rooms in the area surrounding Manchester where, because his real name was unknown, he was catalogued variously as 'The Magistrate', 'Pickwick' or 'The Alderman'. Not until 30 April 1975 was his true identity revealed by a most unfortunate event. The *Daily Telegraph* of that date published a report of the theft from Manchester Cathedral of a brass statuette depicting the Reverend Joshua Brookes, principal character in Mrs Linnaeus Banks's book *The Manchester Man* published in 1876 and long since out of print. Accompanying the report was a photograph of an iron replica of the brass statuette and in every way similar to the fat little man. The search for his name had ended.

▲
236 This 'stiff built' man is said to be known in Sunderland as Robson Weallans, one of the best known solicitors in the area. To others he might look like Bill Sykes and his bull mastif from Dickens's novel, *Oliver Twist*.

A very large number of Victorian notables had their place on mantelshelves of the era, with the Duke of Wellington, often side face to show his famous nose, a favourite example. He was followed closely by Generals Gordon and Wolseley, the former still being remembered for his untimely death but the other, who had a very distinguished career, less well remembered. Characters from Dickens' stories seem to have been almost entirely confined to brass ornaments but ironfounders made use of idealised images of horses, pairs of sheep — a ram and ewe — and dogs of most types although a pair of St Bernards complete with the traditional brandy barrel had a prominent place in their affections. Horses were usually shown in a lively pose indicative of spirit and dash with many of the castings showing a true and detailed appreciation of their beauty. Dogs, too, were mostly well modelled. Other animals such as the cow, pig, elephant (with the exception of Jumbo the famous beast killed by a freight train in St Thomas, Ontario, Canada, on the evening of Tuesday 15 September, 1885) or tiger have never been encountered although they might be expected to be of interest to Victorian designers. However a pair of deer — a stag in a watchful attitude and the hind grazing — are known to exist and were copied by several iron foundries. Small lions, too, were quite popular. Among other interesting mantel ornaments will be found idealised wheatsheaves of various sizes; eagles with outspread wings; (beware of those whose wings have been clipped) and bowls of fruit and flowers but a careful search will be needed and the illustrations show only a small selection of the varieties that were manufactured.

237 Ally and Mrs Sloper, late Victorian comic characters from a paper which featured them in what may have been the first strip cartoon. The marks on their backs, No 119802, show the design to have been registered 16 February 1889 by Richard Row- botham, Providence Foundry, Palmerston Street, Great Ancoats, Manchester. The same firm also cast them in brass.

238 An idealised portrait of a chimney sweep of late Victorian times. 9 in high. ▶

239 This pair of ploughmen, painted in appropriate colours, illustrates Robert Burn's poem *To a mouse on turning her up in her nest with the plough.* The poem contains the following well known words:

but mousie, thou art no thy lane
in proving foresight may be in vain,
the best-laid schemes of mice and men,
gang aft agley....

▼

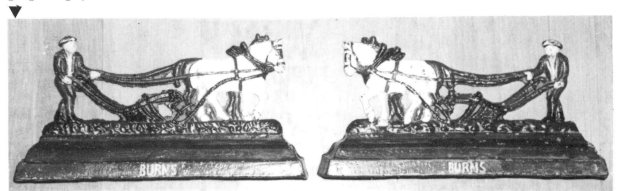

240 A fine pair of castings with much detail. The dogs have been gilded and are bolted to the black bases.

▼

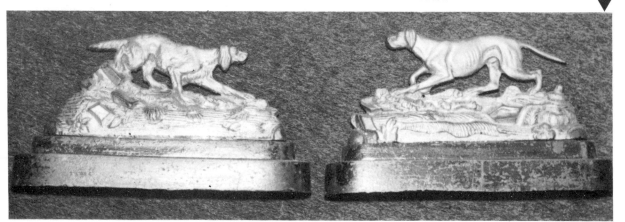

241 Although the story is obscured by corrosion there is no doubt that it is that of the sad tale of the greedy family who, wishing to obtain all their riches at once killed 'the goose that laid the golden eggs' and found they had lost everything by doing so. One of Aesop's fables.

242 Stephenson's *Locomotion* renamed from *Active* ran from Shildon to Stockton via Darlington, County Durham, on September 27, 1825 pulling the earliest public passenger steam train.

7 *Iron for Everything*

In the first chapter, Introducing Cast Iron, mention was made of the Victorian predilection for experimenting with cast iron and how this new raw material with all its attractive properties seems to have been used for practically everything. Ironfounders and their designers could be expected to realise the value of their product in such things as stoves, irons, gates, railings, and as has been said, door furniture, but Victorian imagination and inventiveness went much further. This chapter is therefore a catalogue of a miscellany of items made from cast iron, many of them small or ornate and thus of particular interest to the amateur collector but also included are a few much larger pieces — post boxes, telephone kiosks and road signs for example. These are often only available to public authorities, however, and may seldom or never be collectable by those without large areas of storage space, but since they do represent a sector of the industrial past can be of great interest to folk and other museums. Currently there is an encouraging growth in the type of museum where the displays consist

243 and 244   A fine portrait plaque believed to be Arthur Wellesley, 1st Duke of Wellington. The reverse of the plaque (*right*) shows where the casting was made and by whom.

▼

245 Portrait plaque said to be of
William Ewart Gladstone (1809-
98). Born in Liverpool, he was
four times a liberal reforming
Prime Minister of Great Britain.

246 A cast iron memorial tablet
removed from a church before it
was demolished.

SACRED
TO
THE MEMORY OF
THOMAS APPLEBY.
FOUNDER OF THE
RENISHAW
IRON WORKS.
WHO DEPARTED
LIFE NOV.
AGED 57 YE

of integrated expositions of the way our forefathers lived — village
or city streets complete with an array of shops equipped as they
would have been in the past or dwelling houses of a departed era
and all with furnished rooms. Here the larger cast iron items will
have their place as part of the scene the museum is trying to create.

A list of these collectable items is impressive not only because of
the wide variety of different tasks for which iron was used, but also
because of the diversity of ways in which each individual piece
differed from others made for the same purpose. Cast iron was used
for items including memorial slabs, coat hooks and others as far
separated as street lights and furniture and within each of these
broad classes of function hundreds of design changes took place.
Hat and coat pins for example could, it seems, not be standardised
into perhaps two or three kinds but were made in as many as
thirty-two designs by one foundry alone with others following
closely on its heels; or the ordinary cork squeezer, used by chemists
and others with bottles to fill, could be bought in at least four
highly decorated models. The collector is offered plenty of scope
here. Among other uses to which cast iron was put was in the
manufacture of toys and games, coin operated vending machines
providing chocolate or games of football or even cycle races, as
well as those early 'moving picture' machines showing 'What the
Butler Saw', which could be found for many years on station
platforms and in amusement arcades but have now disappeared
and are forgotten.

As has been described in Chapter 3, Cooking and Keeping Warm, firebacks were among the very earliest uses for cast iron. Probably contemporary with these are graves slabs made in the same way by pouring molten metal into a suitably shaped hollow in a floor of sand making a so called 'flat casting'. Some of these latter, made in the seventeenth and eighteenth centuries, can be found in churches in southern England and they have become quite famous because they have been mentioned by a number of authorities writing about the origins of the foundry trade. So old are these castings that it may come as a surprise to find a basically similar technique being used to turn out vast quantities of useful articles and a few artistic pieces as late as the middle of the twentieth century. Among the most desirable of flat castings are memorial plaques which can be simple in pattern or as elaborate as that of Arthur Wellesley, first Duke of Wellington, which was cast two years after his death in 1852. The design for this plaque was prepared by an unknown artist and the pattern made by a skilled wood carver; the skill required by the team involved in preparing a casting as detailed and elaborate as that of 'The Last Supper', now to be seen in the Coalbrookdale Museum, was of the highest order.

▲
247　One of a pair of circular plaques. The other is inscribed 'Old Lang Syne' with a domestic scene in the centre. This is numbered 5466 and dated 1884.

248　This casting is believed to have been removed, with a companion piece, from the gable ends of an alms house but it is not known when or where.
▼

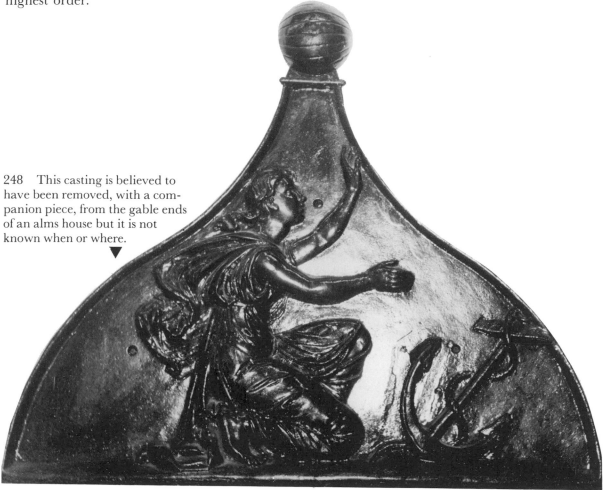

249 The 'Last Supper' in cast iron.

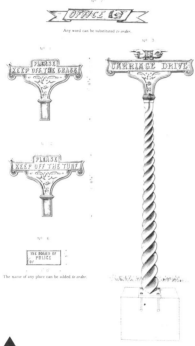

250 Various examples of the many flat informative castings used in streets, parks and on buildings.

In the nineteenth century and during the first half of the twentieth century this same technique of flat casting was adapted as a method of producing all sorts of functional and informative signs. They had a permanence, a resistance to the elements and a clarity difficult to surpass and were very much in favour with local authorities as road signs, finger posts, street names, numbers and what Walter Macfarlane, the Scottish ironfounder of the late nineteenth century, called 'Tablets'. They were used, too, by water authorities, the fire services, by railways and canal management, to convey all sorts of information from the distance to the nearest hydrant to the penalties for trespass. Simple in design, direct in their message, weather resistant and above all, cheap, they could still be decorative and dignified. Their gradual disappearance in favour of pressed steel and plastic is to be deplored for these new materials may do the job more effectively but hardly as pleasantly.

There may be some who consider the inclusion of large items of street furniture such as lamp standards (see Chapter 2 Cast Iron in Architecture) or letter boxes and telephone kiosks in a book of this kind to be stepping outside the strict meaning of the word 'collectable', but there is a clear motive for doing so, which may be an acceptable excuse. All three of these articles are a part of everyday life as we know it now but they are undergoing such radical changes that they may, in the next generation, be completely different from the objects we at present see about us. Indeed the street lamp has already been so simplified as to have no longer any grace or beauty while the letter box, although still made of iron, has also been simplified compared with its early beginnings and although the telephone kiosk has remained much the same, as far as the ordinary observer can tell, since the original design there are now signs of change which it is hoped will make it less easily attacked by vandals. Thus they are all in need of

251   Railway notices are most certainly collectable and much sought after by railway enthusiasts. Notice how the secretary's name has been replaced. This would obviously be necessary, since the life of the cast iron plaque would be far longer than the period during which a secretary would hold his position.

252   Another example of street furniture the purpose of which is to impart information.

253   This posting or pillar box is a standard pillar box designed by the Department of Science and Art and was in use during 1857-9 by the British Postal Service. Made by Smith and Hawkes. (*Post Office Copyright Reserved.*)

254   Designed by J. W. Penfold this posting box was in use from 1866 to 1879. It is six-sided unlike the normal cylindrical models in use at present. It was manufactured by Cockrane & Company and is now at the Ulster Folk Museum, Northern Ireland. (*Post Office Copyright Reserved*).

255   Many streets have, in the past, been named after battles and this cast name plate is in that tradition.

256, 257 and 258   Three bench backs of varying degrees of ornate design from that made to look like a rustic seat to the very intricate lace-like pattern.

259   A somewhat heavy arm chair made by the Coalbrookdale Company and on exhibit in the Ironbridge Gorge Museum.

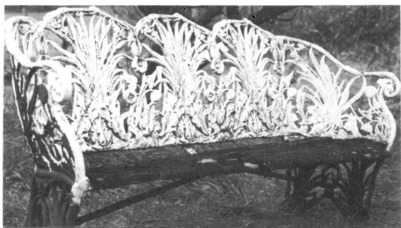

260   A graceful and restrained attempt at making cast iron look like wood. Although it is now black this bench was probably originally painted green.

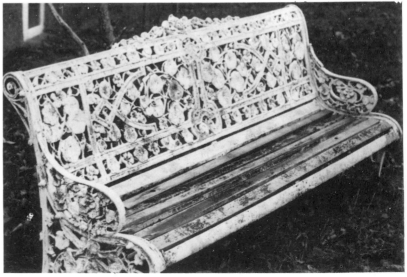

261 One of the most attractive designs for garden seats in cast iron incorporated the fern motif. This fine example is in use at a golf club in Scotland.

preservation and whether by private collectors or by museums matters not.

All collectors of postage stamps are well aware that the first adhesive stamp was issued in Great Britain on the 6 May 1840 but they are less likely to know that it was not until 1852 that the initial experimental roadside pillar box was erected in Britain. Made of cast iron, it was used in Jersey to find out whether the public would accept it. The public did like it but the authorities seemed still to have doubts for the next was put up in Botchergate, Carlisle, Cumbria in 1853 — not as one might expect, in London. The idea caught on and since then there have been a large number of design changes, all in an attempt to make them more effective, eg waterproof, vandal-proof and burglar resistant and to standardise the shape. The result has been to deprive them of much of their early ornamentation, giving rise to the present standard functional type. There are still a number of older boxes in use in Britain going back to Queen Victoria and George V and they are worth looking out for. Some sites are unsuitable for the pillar box and here the Post Office erects either a wall box or a very similar model intended to be attached to a post. Designs for these have changed very little over the years.

262 Typical inn table now used in the garden. It has a female head at the top of each support and paw feet.

Telephone kiosks are almost as ubiquitous as post boxes and they deserve as structures much more attention than they usually receive. Designed by Sir Giles Gilbert Scott in the first quarter of the twentieth century they are good examples of prefabrication — consisting, as they do, of four interlocking and interchangeable sides and a roof. They are reasonably easily transported to the site on which they are to be erected but when bolted together they form a solid and weatherproof unit. Scott's design has stood the test of time having receiving, as far as the layman can see, only minor modifications such as the loss of some ornamental reeding at the corners which was at one time used as reinforcement.

While post boxes and telephone kiosks may be more preservable than collectable, cast iron furniture most certainly has been and still is greatly sought after by collectors. Many ironfounders seem to have offered castings which could either be bolted together to

▲
263 Cannon were very popular toys in the United States and in many other countries. This could be fired with a small charge of gunpowder and might have been in use during Independence Day celebrations on the 4th of July.

▲
264 Admiral Dewey's portrait on this toy cannon — see the 25 cent piece in the foreground — It is a fairly accurate likeness of the Admiral (1837-1917) who defeated the Spanish Fleet at the battle of Manila Bay. He had a long and distinguished service.

▲
265 Also very attractive were pistols in which a tiny measure of gun powder in a paper wrapper could be detonated. Some were repeating and much more ornate but this is a single-shot example.

make a seat or table, or when attached to a wooden seat or top were a complete unit. Unfortunately, because there are few trademarks on the castings identification of the maker is infrequent. Best known of all cast iron furniture is the 'pub' table, consisting, in its original form, of a marble or mahogany top supported by three substantial legs strengthened by a stretcher or circular plate roughly one third of the way to the top. They were deliberately made solid and heavy so they could not easily be used as weapons in a brawl. One type was even designed to be bolted to the floor. Some had Britannia with her shield at the top of the leg and thus were named 'Britannia' tables but others had a ram's head or a female face in place of the patriotic motif. Paws, claws and cloven hooves were used as feet. Park and other benches and chairs, of course, are much sought after not only because they are collectable but also because they are so useful.

In the 'good old days' when thrift closely followed Godliness and cleanliness as the most desirable of human virtues our ironfounders were pleased to assist in teaching their worth. The acquisitive child was greatly aided in the accumulation of wealth by all sorts of interesting small banks made of cast iron and some of these were made to swallow the saver's coins at the press of a lever, while others were inscribed with a suitable maxim such as 'Every Copper Helps'. Many of these banks have survived all attempts to get at their contents by violent means and are avidly pursued by collectors. Although some were made by British firms there is a possibility they were copying designs produced in the USA where they were manufactured in vast numbers. Toy money banks fall into three quite distinct categories. 'Still' banks where there was no reward for saving other than a satisfying 'clink' as the coin fell to the bottom were the simplest and probably the first. These are fairly common and may be replicas of buildings, houses, animals, prominent people or comic strip characters. They could also take the form of an iron safe and some had combination locks.

Much more attractive, and sought after, are mechanical banks as these offered action of some kind or other as incentive for the young saver. At least 300 different varieties of these are known to have been marketed between 1869 when John Hall patented his Excelsior Bank and 1910 when inventiveness and manufacture began to decline. A third type, although not usually of cast iron, was the Register Bank. Shaped like a cash register it 'rang up' the amount of money on deposit. Portrait banks which could be both still and mechanical were great favourites both with the designer and the customer. Among these is General Benjamin F. Butler as a green-backed frog. In 1884 the General was a US Presidential candidate and his platform advocated 'green-backs'. President Theodore Roosevelt was caricatured as a bear hunter who fired a coin from his rifle into a bear. Sometimes the rifle could be fitted with a cap and made a satisfying noise as the coin disappeared. Teddy as a lion hunter and one believed to show General Grant dropping a coin into a barrel are much rarer. Other conspicious people or characters whose likenesses appeared as banks are

266 When this toy was pulled along the floor the oarsmen would row. No indication of maker.

267 A pull toy battle ship listed by the Shelburne Museum as the gunboat *Kearsarge* and dated about 1890. There were two American ships of this name. This appears to be the earlier one which destroyed a Confederate cruiser in 1864.

268 This pull toy bears little similarity to a Mississippi river steam boat.

269 The *City of New York* is a paddle-wheel steamer and when this model is pulled the walking beam to the right of the paddles moves up and down. Believed to be c1890.

270 Very similar to 269 but called *Puritan*, the means by which motion was transferred to the walking beam is shown more clearly.

271 Another kind of pull toy, this has a bell which is sounded by a hammer at the left. On the other side of the carriage are the words 'Landing of Columbus'.

272 In winter, in the past, transport was often by horse-drawn sleigh. This elegant pull toy was a miniature of the real thing. The figure of a driver is missing as shown by the hole in the seat by which it was attached.

273 In this pull toy representing a cab (but minus the driver) the horse has a skid at its foot to which the string was attached. Some horses were made so that their legs moved when they were dragged along the ground.

274 Ice was delivered from door to door in summer. This miniature ice-waggon has lost its driver.

275 An American 25 cent coin (about the size of a 5p piece) shows how small these two toys are. On the right we have Santa Claus in his sleigh pulled by reindeer, an ever popular theme. ▼

276 Although this looks like a pull toy it is in fact a money bank. It is called the 'Bad Accident' bank. A coin is inserted under the driver and when a catch is released the little black boy dashes from behind the bush, frightens the mule which rears up and pushes the coin into the bank beneath the driver.

277 Mules were standard draught animals in parts of the United States and so they are often used in pull toys like this.

278 Daisy must have been designed for the females of the family. She has a rather simple expression on her face as, for that matter, do many of the dolls of the era.

279 Made by the N. N. Hill Brass Company this toy, which is believed to be of iron, rang the bell as it moved because the clapper was free to move.

280 Model fire equipment had a fascination for children more than all other toys of the era, thus large numbers were sold and many examples survive.

281 Water pressure for the hoses was raised by steam and this 'steam pumper' is one of many different designs available.

282 The theme is the same but the detail different. It looks as if there were one or two riders at the rear when the toy was new.

106

283 Hose wagons, of which this is one, were part of the fire appliance collection. Here, the hose has disappeared, but the toothed wheel which rang a bell can be seen.

284 Another hose wagon, this time with the hose but the rider at the rear of the appliance has gone. No bell on this design.

285 Ladder trucks, too, were needed to complete the equipment. Spirited horses were fitted to all these fire equipment toys.

286 This is a large pull toy as it is 31 in long.

287 A different method of ringing the fire-bell can be seen here. All these fire appliance toys are from the early part of the twentieth century.

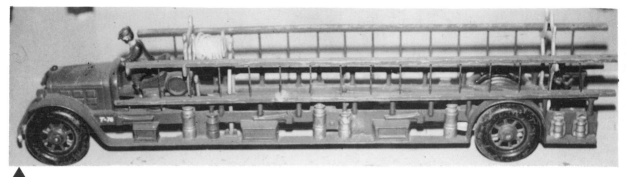

288 Although motorised fire appliances became popular those pulled by horses remained in great demand for many years after they were no longer used by fire departments.

General Pershing, Franklin Delano Roosevelt, Boss Tweed, Mutt and Jeff, Aunt Jemima, Punch and Judy, William Tell, Humpty Dumpty and Jonah and the Whale. Most mechanical banks were of cast iron and many had highly complex mechanisms. Hall's Exclesior Bank (patented in 1869) had a figure, either a man or monkey, and a table which rose from beneath the hinged roof, which was lifted by pulling the doorbell. The weight of a coin placed on the table deposited the coin and closed the roof. John Hall also patented the Race Course Bank — dropping a coin into the bank caused horses to run around a circular track, and the Tammany Bank where a child's savings, placed on Boss Tweed's right hand caused it to fall and the money went into his pocket. There were several designs where a cashier appeared to receive and deposit a coin on opening the door of the bank.

Banks with descriptive or amusing slogans such as 'Always did 'Spise a Mule', 'Every Copper Helps', an egg bank with 'My Nest Egg', 'Good Luck', or a pig described as 'A Christmas Roast' and many others have been found by collectors. One particular slogan bank is mentioned in *Antique Metalware*. It was patented in 1870 and here the coin caused one of four captions to appear in a slot over the door — 'Give Me A Penny', 'Thank You', 'One More', 'Do So Again'. Most of these cast iron banks were painted in bright colours to resemble the object that was being represented, but there was a fashion for some to be silvered or bronzed. Known manufacturers were Stevens and Hubley of Lancaster, Pennsylvania, but to only ten of over 120 banks examined by the author could a manufacturer be ascribed. Very few have a maker's name in the casting although a great many do bear patent dates. Collectors will find few old banks without signs of severe wear — damaged parts, faded or chipped paint or restored mechanisms — nevertheless prices are high and going higher. A recent review of the USA market showed good mechanical banks at up to $400 (£200) and still banks as high as $100 (£50). These same objects will have been sold wholesale at $2.50 to $5 a dozen (20-40 cents (10-20p) *each*) eighty years ago.

There seems to be little doubt that most cast iron playthings were created by men to be toys for boys. There may have been some which appealed to females, but they were of a domestic type more to train the little girl in her future duties than to amuse. Some

289 As an added concession to realism this pump truck has rubber tyres.

290 Here is a combined pumper and hose wagon to which is attached all the extra equipment needed to fight the fire.

291 The train set has always been popular. This observation car, with its platform at its rear, comes from a complete train consisting of a steam engine *No 70 Keystone Express*, and cars with names like *604 Celtic*, *605 Ivanhoe* and of course *606 Hypatia*. (See Fig 294.)

292 This electric-type locomotive is much younger than the passenger car with the letters CPRR. (Possibly Canadian Pacific Rail Road).

293 Although the legend reads 'pat Jun 8 1880' this locomotive could have been made many years later. There is no means of telling its age.

294 This is the locomotive to which the car illustrated in Fig 291 was attached.

of the masculine kinds would have had an interest for some of the 'Tom Boy' persuasion, but on the whole their charm was for the male child. A vast majority of the toys made of cast iron were intended to be pulled, or pushed, along the nursery floor and seldom had moving parts, except for revolving wheels. They came in sizes extending from the miniature to models of an elaborate nature a foot or more in length. Among the most popular were horse-drawn fire appliances — steam pumpers, hook and ladder rigs, horse carts, chief's wagons and water towers, some of which were equipped to squirt water in a realistic manner. They continued in production until the first quarter of the twentieth century at least.

All forms of transport were miniaturised to make pull toys: railway engines, tenders, passenger and freight cars — whole sets of railway rolling stock could be coupled together — and there were, too, horse drawn coaches and even coal and ice wagons. At a later stage as the internal combusion engine became better known, horses were replaced by motorised vehicles. Replicas of early firetrucks and other fire-fighting equipment were produced. Then came automobiles, taxis, delivery trucks, lorries, and even ambulances in their thousands. Perhaps as popular as any other pull-toy was the circus wagon and all that went with it to make a parade. Painted in bright colours they had a wide appeal and came in sets consisting of animals in a cage, wagons, band wagons, vehicles carrying clowns and some with a steam organ. Another kind of pull toy which enjoyed a considerable vogue was the bell toy. When drawn across the floor a bell was rung or chimes played and these could be of cast iron although they were also made of other materials.

295 Although much like the engine shown in Fig 293 it is not exactly the same. There is no patent date. The letters on the passenger car are WHIST and the tender is number 976.

296 A pretty cast iron weighing balance, but only one weight remains.

297 Dolls and doll's houses needed furnishing and iron-founders/toy makers were pleased to oblige with pot, pans and irons as well as many other items.

298 More miniature household equipment for the doll's house.

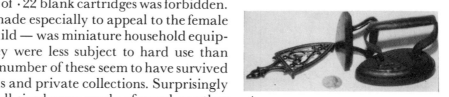

299 Toy irons and iron stands for the young house-wife were made in thousands. The 25 cent piece gives an indication of the size.

In *Tha Handbook of Old American Toys* L. H. Hertz describes three cast iron toys which must have been irresistible to the young male — cannon, cap pistols and bombs. Cannon, for celebrations such as Independence Day, were pretty realistic. They were filled with gunpowder and exploded by means of a fuse and some could make a most satisfactory 'bang', although those only 3 inches long would have been somewhat disappointing. Others were made to take a fire cracker and others to explode a cap. Cap pistols, both single shot and repeating, were much coveted by the young man disguised as a cowboy or an Indian and manufacturers gave them a substantial choice including replicas of the real thing. They also made a line of unrealistic but attractive items where moving figures ornamented the mechanism. The sole purpose of these was to explode the cap by kicking, bucking, falling or some other suitable action when the trigger was pulled. One particularly lethal type is described by L. H. Hertz. It is a pistol made to hold a fire cracker where on explosion of the cracker a clown seated on a barrel flies off in the direction of the person holding the toy. Cap-exploding bombs, well remembered by the author, consisted of cast iron replicas of a bomb, a human head or that of an animal, on a string, would, when dropped, explode a cap inserted in the mechanism. These were very satisfactory, but the bomb described as suitable for the explosion of ·22 blank cartridges was forbidden.

The sort of cast iron toy made especially to appeal to the female market — both adult and child — was miniature household equipment. Perhaps because they were less subject to hard use than those made for boys a large number of these seem to have survived and can be seen in museums and private collections. Surprisingly many pieces which when full sized were made of wood or other materials were produced in miniature in cast iron — chests of drawers, sofas, seats, chairs, tables or mirrors can all be found. There were also tiny sad irons, washing machines, ironing boards, iron stands, cooking stoves complete with pots and pans ready to delight the growing girl and to furnish her doll's house. Stoves were very common and like sad irons often bear the name of a maker of the full sized article. Some of the early sewing machines were copied in cast iron as toys. Allied to this class of plaything

111

▲

300   This toy range comes complete with pots and pans and a stove-lid lifter.

▲

301   The 'Gem' miniature range even has a coal scuttle and shovel.

were the so-called 'Penny Toys'. Made to sell at very low prices they were tiny models of garden tools, hammers, hatchets, coal scuttles and other common objects. They have become rather scarce either because they were of such low value or because they are so small.

There is some basis for the claim made by some authors that the manufacturers of cast iron banks and toys in the United States led the world in quality, quantity and inventiveness. The most important American name in the business was that of Ives of Bridgeport (1868-1932) Connecticut. This firm was renowned for the design and quality of their castings and it is said that many of the toys *claimed* to be of Ives manufacture would not have been fit for their scrap heap. Unfortunately, not many of their products are identifiable with certainty, although some clues are of help. Ives line of cast iron toys included pull toys of most kinds, clockwork toys including both trackless and tracked railway train sets, cannon of all three kinds — gunpowder, fire cracker and blank cartridge, and cap pistols. They used cast iron for parts of toys such as electric trains but they are not known as large makers of money banks. Incidentally, the name Ives crops up as an ironfounder in Montreal, Canada. Other great names in the cast iron toy trade are Carpenter, Hubley, Weeden, Stevens of Cromwell, Connecticut and there are of course, others. The subject of collectable cast iron toys has been given much attention by researchers and there are a number of books worth reading so the foregoing can only be an indication of the scope for collectors. Prices will be found to range from $10 or $11 (£5-£5.50) for shooting gallery chickens to more than $400 (£200) for a circus wagon. Stoves can be had for from $50 to $150 (£25-£75) and locomotives and train sets bring from $30 to $300 (£15-£150) depending on condition and number of pieces.

The final paragraphs of this chapter will truly indicate that cast iron was indeed used for everything — or almost. The articles now to be described might be called 'Odd Work', to steal a phrase from one ironfounder's catalogue. First there were hat and coat pins made by Baldwin, Son & Co. They were all very ornate and might, if the illutrations are accurate, have caused damage both to the clothing they supported and the fingers of those using them. Spitoons are no longer much used, but used to be shown in many ironfounder's catalogues. The illustrations show other small items all attractive to the collector. Stationer's sundries too, offer scope for those who wish to start an easily displayed selection or it may be that photograph frames, clock stands, ink stands or book ends will prove to have most appeal for some collectors.

◀ 302   Another toy range called the 'Ark'.

303 After the advent of gas stoves they were also provided as toys for the young. In this illustration there is also an early model clothes washing machine with a hand wringer.

304 This group consisting of a rocker, a range and a sledge is of iron.

305 Children enjoyed a very wide selection of toy household items for their make-believe lives, as this collection indicates.

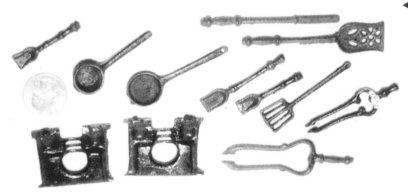

306 This could have been a salesman's sample grate although it is exhibited as a toy.

▲

307 These money boxes were manufactured by John Harper. The subject matter of some would certainly be frowned upon by race relations authorities today.

308 One of the earliest patents for a cast iron mechanical money bank was taken out by J. Hall on 21 December 1869 for his Excelsior Bank. When the door knob was pulled the top was raised and a little monkey comes up with a table on which the coin is rested. The weight of the coin reverses the action while the coin falls into the bank. American.

▶

The articles illustrated also support the thought that cast iron was used for everything and most of it is collectable. The decoration on the device used to impress an official seal to prove their authenticity on documents issued by local authorities, banks and other institutions has much attraction. These seal presses usually had a pin secured by a lock to prevent unofficial use. Other presses of this kind were used to emboss an address to a letterhead. Cast iron insects with different uses are also shown. The house fly has wings which can be lifted to reveal matches kept in the body, safe, dry and handy on the stove or on a shelf while the other two are different versions of the stag beetle intended for use as boot jacks where the boot heel is inserted between the horns, the other foot put on the body and the foot removed from the boot by a strong pull. This kind of casting was very popular on the Continent and is still being made. The crucifix may be the only known example although there are known to have been painted altar-pieces, with a crucifix and candlesticks of cast iron and finished in electro brass or bronze. There was also a cast iron altar-piece exhibited by J. M. Bennett at the Manchester Royal Jubilee Exhibition of 1887.

The plant stand or the ornamental miniature urn and a tobacco jar will also interest collectors. The tobacco jar was cast by Crowley of Manchester and Sheffield from a pattern carved by Stevens in the nineteenth century. This Stevens may have been Alfred Stevens (1818-75) who did so much to erase the worst flamboyant excesses of Victorian design and who, it has been said, turned cast iron into a 'lady'. Also illustrated are two cannon, a type of casting which ranks with grave slabs and firebacks as among the most ancient of casting arts. The first is a toy or decoration but the other, salvaged from a moat surrounding Caerlaverock Castle, Dumfrieshire, Scotland during some repairs may have been capable of being fired in anger although it is not known whether it was.

309 An example of an English still money bank designed to attract spare cash from Victorian children. The motto 'Every Copper Helps' was, of course, also intended to teach those same children that the police were there to assist rather than to punish. He is 6in high.

310 A modern still bank about 4in high. Canadian.

311 This conventional still bank is about sixty or more years old.

312 Magic banks are mechanical. When the front door is opened a figure of a teller appears, takes your money and disappears. ▶

313 When offered a coin some of these Bull Dog banks snatch it from the fingers but this one only swallows the coin with a shake of its head when his tail is pulled. Made by Stevens and dated 27 April 1880 but may be much later.

314 Wise Old Owl bank. The coin is placed in an opening on the owl's left. On pushing a lever the head turns pushing the coin into the bank. On some the eyes move. Stevens, 28 Sept 1880.

315 Uncle Sam bank. Place the coin in his hand, pull a lever and the coin is placed in his carpet bag, which opens to receive it, and his whiskers move. 8 June 1886.

316 Trick Dog bank. On using a lever the dog jumps through the hoop and deposits a coin from its mouth into the barrel.

317 The Organ Bank is one of the more complicated mechanical banks. When a coin is deposited and the handle turned the dog and cat dance around, the monkey doffs his hat and a chime of bells can be heard. About 5in by 3in by 5in high it bears the inscription 13 Jan 1882, 259403.

318 Dark Town Battery is a bank with a base ball theme. The coin is placed in the pitcher's hand and when a lever is operated he throws the coin at the batsman who strikes at it, misses, and as the catcher fails to hold it the coin falls into the hole between his legs.

319 With this Magic bank a coin is placed under the hat which, when lowered by the magician, causes it to disappear. The biggest mystery about these banks is how one retrieved the money when the bank was full.

320 This is a Creedmore bank in which the soldier fires the coin from his rifle into the tree trunk. Named after an old New York State rifle range on Long Island.

321 Called a William Tell bank the coin is fired from the rifle, hits the apple on the boy's head and falls into the tree. A paper cap can be fitted to the rifle in both these banks to give a realistic noise when the gun was fired. Also called the Tyrolese bank. Stevens, 23 June 1896.

322 Instead of swallowing Jonah the whale takes the coin which is tossed into its mouth from the tray held by Jonah.

323 The Bear Hunt bank. The Indian shoots a coin into the bear's chest when the plunger is pushed. Stevens, 17 Jan 1888. At least one variation was sold with a figure of 'Teddy' Roosevelt instead of the Indian.

324 Mules and Negroes were favourite subjects for inventors of mechanical banks. Called 'Always did 'Spise a Mule' bank the mule rears up, the jockey is thrown over his head and the coin which is in the jockey's mouth falls into the bank. Stevens, 22 April 1879.

326 Politicians were often caricatured in banks. This is a Boss Tweed bank. William Marcy Tweed (1823-78) was boss of the Tammany General Committee which had complete power in New York City. He was jailed in 1873 for two years, released and again imprisoned, escaped to Cuba then to Spain but was recaptured and died in jail. His dishonesty is commemorated in this bank where a coin placed in his hand falls into his pocket.

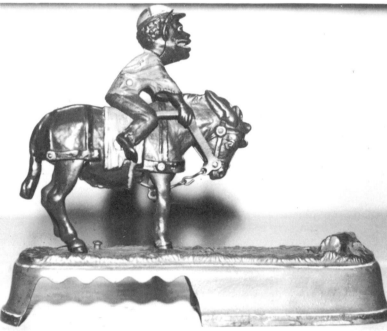

325 The American Eagle bank was activated by a lever which caused a coin in the mother eagle's beak to fall into the nest whereupon mother flapped her wings the little birds opened their mouths and chirped. The noise is produced by a bellows. Stevens, 23 (?) 1883. Patented by Charles M. Henn.

119

327 A small selection of the many spittoons cast in iron. They were in common use in the latter part of the nineteenth and early twentieth centuries.

No. 12   No. 13   No. 14

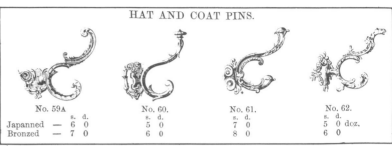

HAT AND COAT PINS.

	No. 59A	No. 60.	No. 61.	No. 62.
	s. d.	s. d.	s. d.	s. d.
Japanned —	6 0	5 0	7 0	5 0 doz.
Bronzed —	7 0	6 0	8 0	6 0

FIG. H.

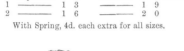

NEW CORK SQUEEZER.
No. 3.

		s. d.	
Japanned	———	1 6	each
Bronzed	———	2 0	

FIG. I.

CORK SQUEEZERS.

No.	Japanned	s. d.		Bronzed	s. d.	
0	Japanned	1 0		Bronzed	1 6	each.
1	———	1 3		———	1 9	
2		1 6		———	2 0	

With Spring, 4d. each extra for all sizes.

FIG. K.

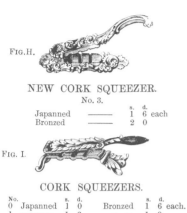

SUGAR NIPPERS.

330 Once upon a time cork squeezers were in constant use by bottlers, pharmacists and chemists as a means of making the cork fit the bottle neck. When sugar was sold in lump form the sugar nippers were used to break the pieces down to usable size. These small castings were among what Archibald Kenrick called 'Odd Work' in their 1871-3 catalogue.

328 Ornate coat and hat hooks or 'pins' as they are also called. They are seldom seen nowadays but would make an interesting and useful collection.

329 These examples of stationer's sundries show how much there is to collect if one keeps one's eyes open.

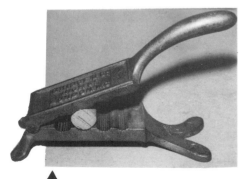

331 A real cork squeezer still in use in a chemist's shop.

332 Plug tobacco was frequently sold in village shops especially in the USA. This instrument was used to cut small pieces off the large plug for sale to customers. Why the customer was treated to the sight of a little man thumbing his nose is a mystery.

333 Balls of string were placed in these cages from which lengths could easily and conveniently be drawn.

334 This string dispenser hangs from the ceiling or some other support.

335 A paper weight in the shape of the 'Legs of Man'.

336 This is a 'country' made paper weight but it has a certain dignity.

337 This is a match safe to be hung on the wall.

121

338 Cast iron candle holder in the form of a leaf.

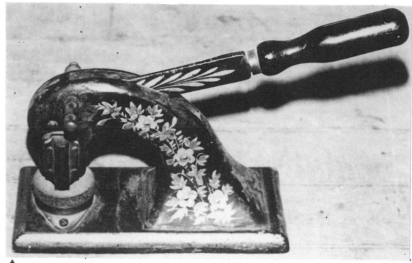

339 Official seals were pressed into documents by instruments like this decorated example. As is usual it is fitted with a pin which can be locked in place so the press cannot be used by unauthorised persons.

340 Another and more utilitarian example of the same kind of press. The pin and lock can be seen here very clearly.

342 This cast iron base for a table has an arrangement by which the table top can be raised or lowered.

341 A clock in a cast iron case. It was made in the United States.

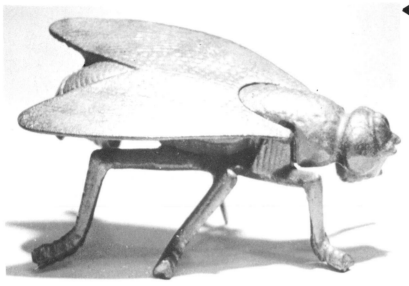

343 A match safe. Lift the wings of the house fly and in its body will be found matches to light the fire. It was often kept on top of the stove or range where the contents would be safe and dry. Made in Quebec, Canada.

344 and 345 Creatures of this kind, in this instance stag beetles, are a favourite model for boot jacks in many countries. The heel of the shoe or boot is put between the antenna and the other foot placed on the body to hold it firm. A gentle pull should then withdraw the foot from the boot.

347 She is called 'Naughty Nellie' and she is very often reproduced today. A better name for her might be 'Silly Susan' — what woman would allow a man to put his foot on her face and his heel between her legs?

346 This is an American made boot jack.

348 An altar piece made of cast iron. These are most uncommon.

349 This 9in high urn with a cover has no known use except possibly to hold someone's ashes.

350 An unusual tobacco jar in cast iron. It was cast by Crowley of Manchester and Sheffield (see Fig 231) from a carving by Stevens in the nineteenth century. This Stevens may have been the same man who is credited with having turned cast iron into a 'Lady'.

351 An iron eagle — eagles made of all types of material are frequently seen in the United States.

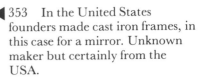

353 In the United States founders made cast iron frames, in this case for a mirror. Unknown maker but certainly from the USA.

352 A cast iron photograph frame. Rather clumsily ornate objects like this are the sort of item greatly sought after by collectors as they are small and could be thought visually quite attractive.

354 A cast iron photograph frame, gilded and now used to frame an arrangement of dried flowers.

355 There is much cast iron used in this old fine double cheese press from the late nineteenth century. It is decorated with the coat of arms of Queen Victoria and scenes from the cheese-making trade. From Bishop Hooper's Lodgings, Gloucester.

356 In the early days in the northern United States and Canada it was the custom to roll snow to make roads passable. Now it is removed by a plough. This is a horse pulled snow roller — mostly of wood but with iron fittings.

357 Avery, who made this cast iron machine for giving change for gold sovereigns believe there is only one other in existence.

358 Old sewing machines, which are mainly made of cast iron have become collector's pieces.

359 This example of an old sewing machine shows how well they were finished and why they are collectable.

360 An even earlier sewing machine.

361 One of a pair of cast iron urns, made into flower planters. They were under water in a river for twenty-five years. It is in good condition, illustrating the power of cast iron to withstand the elements.

362 Impressive old iron urns far more durable and sightly than the plastic objects that are offered today.

363 Iron urns are sought after for garden use, and are now becoming expensive.

364 and 365 The lion and the unicorn traditionally associate with each other on coats of arms and in other places such as toppings for park gates. They are greatly sought after by collectors and are now reproduced. This is a pair and thus much more important.

367 The body of this cork screw in the shape of a tortoise is cast iron.

366 Even the museum staff have no idea what this cast iron object is. It must have had some use for it was patented 12 July 1857 by H. Johnson.

368 A collection of horse equipment. Hitching weights to keep the team from wandering off and the top from a hitching post in the shape of a horse's head. The horse shoes are made of wrought iron.

369 and 370 Two hitching posts, these were most popular in the United States. The one on the left bears the name John McCann.

371 At the time when horse-drawn vehicles were in use they were kept in wooden barns in the United States. When carts were being removed there was a danger that wheels and hubs would wear or smash the wooden posts. This is a casting fixed to such a post. When a wheel came too near it was kept away by the shape of the protective hoof and leg. There were two to each post.

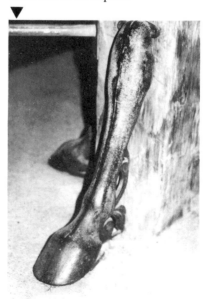

8 Collecting, Cleaning and Display

Nowadays, whatever it is that one starts to collect it seems as if everyone else has already been hoarding the same thing for years. Consequently prices are high, supply limited and competition fierce. Nor is there much scope for discovery of new facts — the whole subject has been debated, discussed, investigated and written about until it seems thoroughly worked out and little more can be learned. Some surprise in the form of an important find, such as turning up a treasure of old coins, is always possible and happens with astonishing frequency but the chances are small. The majority of attics, cellars and other likely places of shelter for a painting, some pieces of silver, good furniture or some other well-established type of connoisseur's pleasure have been explored thoroughly. In other words a windfall is improbable.

Collectors of cast iron, however, are not faced with the same problems. The field, relatively speaking, is largely unexplored. Antique shops, auction sales, antique fairs, scrap merchants, church bazaars and even the town refuse tip are still able to offer their quota. Admittedly folk and other museums have acquired large amounts of old cast iron — a good deal of which remains hidden from public view, but the general public is now beginning to take more interest and at the same time there is more realisation of its decorative value. This is beneficial in that preservation is ensured, but so great was the output of ironfounders that there is still no dearth of exciting prizes to be won by even the most casual search. On the other hand resolution in the hunt can bring rewards; much cast iron will be found in unexpected locations or in unusual applications. For cast iron is not always obvious — it may have been disguised or used in a deceiving way. An example would be those impressive Doric columns usually associated with wood, concrete, Portland stone or marble. They may be of iron and the use of a magnet is a cheap and effective detector.

Nor is the investigation ended when the article has been procured. Much can be learned of the history, use, by whom it was manufactured and how best it may be cleaned and displayed. Very often, unfortunately, castings have no identification mark of any kind and so are destined to remain anonymous unless of course their provenance can be established either by word of mouth or by some document. These are somewhat less valuable and very much less interesting than those carrying either a registration mark or the makers name or, with luck, both.

Before 1842, and indeed quite often afterwards, it was not

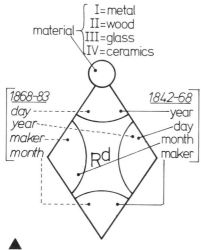

372 The registration mark used to date articles.

unknown for one firm to copy designs from another. This form of piracy was thought to be unfair and so a scheme whereby an article could be registered with the British Patent Office, and thus protected for three years, was created. It commenced in the year 1842 and manufacturers whose products were registered used a distinctive mark — called a lozenge — consisting of a triangle, a circle and quadrants of a circle in each of the four corners together with a system of letters and numbers. From 1842 to 1868 starting from the top of the triangle and moving clockwise the code could be read as follows: top circle is the type of material (1 means metal); under the circle is the year; right quadrant is the day; bottom is the parcel from which the maker's name can be ascertained by search of the appropriate records, and left is the month. From 1868 to 1883 when the system was abandoned in favour of numbers the sequence was changed to: top — day, right — year, bottom — month, and left — parcel. Letter codes were:

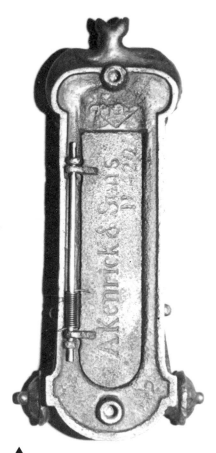

373 The reverse of the Kenrick knocker in Fig 140. The lozenge at the top, although almost obliterated, indicates that the design was registered in 1880. This is supported by the fact that the name A. Kenrick & Sons was used from 1830 to 1882 after which it was changed to A. Kenrick & Sons Ltd.

Years

1842 — X — 1868	1849 — S — 1875	1856 — L — 1882	1863	G
1843 — H — 1869	1850 — V — 1876	1857 — K — 1883	1864	N
1844 — C — 1870	1851 — P — 1877	1858	B	1865	W
1845 — A — 1871	1852 — D — 1878	1859	M	1866	Q
1846 — I — 1872	1853 — Y — 1879	1860	Z	1867	T
1847 — F — 1873	1854 — J — 1880	1861	R		
1848 — U — 1874	1855 — E — 1881	1862	O		

Months

Jan	C	April	H	July	I	Oct	B
Feb	G	May	E	Aug	R	Nov	K
Mar	W	June	M	Sept	D	Dec	A

From the above it will be seen that the ash guard in Fig 376 was registered on 16 August 1880 by Chas Ezard, the dog (Fig 375) on 24 February 1858. Registration marks are no guarantee of age. Given the original pattern — and they were almost indestructible — manufacture could continue for many, many years. The change to a number system — four or more digits following the symbol Rd — is much less satisfactory to the investigator who can obtain no details without recourse to the Public Records Office either personally or on payment of a fee. Three figures on the back of some castings are likely to be the catalogue number of the manufacturer, not to be confused with Registration. Fig 374 shows the reverse of two Kenrick patterns with their catalogue numbers. Notice also holes into which handles were fixed to make removal of the patterns from the mould easier.

Dating the actual casting is full of pitfalls and the collector must beware since forgeries or recent copies are extremely difficult to detect. Manufacturers' catalogues can be of some use but they are very limited in their utility as is indicated in the following example. Fig 373 is the reverse of the combined letter slot and knocker shown in Fig 140 which appeared in Kenrick's catalogue for 1880, but it

374 Two casting patterns for the Kenrick door porter, model 454 with both long and short handles. These were castings made from the first wooden patterns carved from the designer's drawings; they were cleaned up and used in the moulding shop to make moulds for production castings. Note the holes in the back into which handles could be screwed. With these handles the pattern could be withdrawn with a minimum of disturbance. To the non-expert they are indistinguishable from a production casting.

was still there in 1926 and the knocker itself continues in use to this day. It was, however, probably made in about 1900, judging from the age of the house on which it was found. Another possible way of dating designs is through trade marks. For example, through the years Kenrick's mark developed as follows:

1791 — A. Kenrick
1811 to 1827 — A. Kenrick & Co
1828 — A. Kenrick & Son
1830 to 1882 — A. Kenrick & Sons
1883 to date — A. Kenrick & Sons Ltd

Thus we know the *pattern* for our door knocker (but not necessarily the item itself) was made between 1830 and 1882 even without the benefit of a catalogue. Changes in trade marks by other iron-founders have not yet been investigated but could prove a useful exercise. For example Carron Company had at least three and possibly four marks in use over the years.

Is cleaning advisable? A question frequently asked and one to which there are several answers. On the whole, and unless too much detail has been obscured by paint, blacklead or corrosion, there seems to be a good case for leaving well alone. For one thing thorough cleaning involves a chemical treatment in which *all* surface coatings, and not only accumulated dirt, are removed including the original finish. Ironfounders seem to have had only four finishes — Japan black, Berlin black, electro-brass and antique bronze and the last three are very difficult to imitate as the following directions will serve to show. Of course large architectural castings would have been painted according to a client's instructions which might have involved a green usually based on Brunswick green pigment, which turned blue when exposed to an industrial atmosphere.

Japan black, a shiny, brittle and not very durable coating appears, according to one old recipe book, to have been formulated using twelve ounces of amber and two ounces of asphaltum fused by heating and to which is added half a pint of boiled oil and two ounces of rosin. While cooling sixteen ounces of oil of turpentine were added and the varnish was then ready for use. Berlin black gave a tougher, more durable and possibly less brilliant black than Japanning and was obtained by heating after application. The electro brass effect could have been achieved by electrical deposition on the casting of copper and zinc from an aqueous bath of their salts. Antique bronze may have been a trade secret although the old recipe book tells how it could be made by allowing the cleaned casting to stand in the vapour of a mixture of concentrated hydrochloric and nitric acids. It is then wiped over with a thin film of vaseline and heated until the vaseline begins to decompose. The author has tried none of these formulae and so is unsure of the result of any of these 'recipes'.

375 Reverse of the door porter in Fig 168 showing the registration mark and the pattern number 19.

376 Reverse of the 'Tidy Betty' shown in Fig 45. The maker's or designer's name was Chas Ezard and the design was registered on 16 August 1880, as shown by the lozenge.

377 This is how the Shelburne Museum displays a part of its collection of irons by attaching them to peg board. As they are wired to the board there is little danger from pilfering.

Although the collector will frequently come upon small items of cast iron that have been decorated with coloured paints there is insufficient evidence from catalogues to suggest that this was done by the manufacturers. Money banks were advertised as hand painted in natural colours but apart from these the author is firmly of the opinion that all door porters and chimney ornaments were sold black or bronzed and that paint was applied by the owners when the original finish became time-worn. Some, such as door porters representing Scottish soldiers are more attractive when painted and it would be a pity to make them revert to their original state. The short answer seems to be that if they are painted let them stay that way.

Much the simplest way to deal with small castings if they are in reasonable condition is to touch up the paint with very dull colours or when they are black to polish them with Zebrite black-lead or black boot polish. If however complete cleaning is necessary then collectors are advised to find a co-operative engineering firm with equipment to remove all surface dirt and to shot or sand blast afterwards. Small items can no doubt be treated at home by boiling in a 10 per cent solution of caustic soda in an iron, never aluminium, pan until most of the rust, paint or black-lead has been loosened. Then use a knife or sharp pointed instrument to perform the tedious business of cleaning all the tiny chinks and crevices. This action should be followed by adding a protective coating of black-lead, black or bronze lacquer or coloured paint as desired. Black-lead or black paint is recommended unless the artist is very skilful, for otherwise the new colours will look garish and out of place for a long time.

About display little can be said since so much depends on the size and type of collection, on whether one lives in a small or large house or whether one is a museum curator or not. At Castle Museum, York the collection of door porters and chimney ornaments was, when last seen, mounted on a wall at the end of a

378 Part of the author's collection displayed on a specially constructed chimney and fireplace.

379 Boot jacks on display at Shelburne Museum where they are safe from light fingers but can be seen by all.

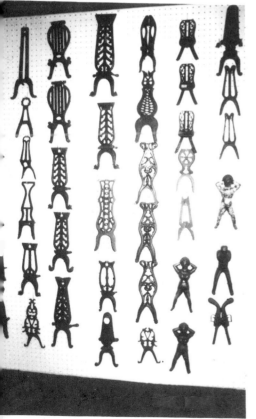

large gallery — an effective setting. Some folk museums have a room or rooms furnished as an ironmonger's shop — surely a most authentic setting. Part of the author's collection is displayed on steps built into the chimney above an open fire and another collector has his on shelves built just above floor level around a large room. Shelves just below ceiling level make a very satisfactory frieze if ornamented with choice pieces in much the same way that plates are displayed.

Quite the most enterprising display is that in a barn specially adapted for the purpose because the collector's wife objected to having it in the house. Howsoever the collection is housed there is one piece of advice to be heeded: cast iron is heavy and it is brittle. Glass shelves are to be avoided at all costs and if shelves are to be built make very sure they are firmly fixed, for a fall could have a shattering effect.

Museums Displaying Cast Iron

A selection of museums in Britain and America where collectable cast iron may be seen.

Fire Plates, Fire Backs and Stoves

Anne of Cleves House, High Street, Southover, Lewes, England
Antique Stove Museum, Hoosick, New York, USA
Bucks County Historical Society, Doylestown, Pa, USA
Essex Institute, Salem, Massachusetts, USA
Hamilton Historical Society, Carlisle, Pa, USA
Mercer Museum, Doylestown, Pa, USA
Pennsylvania State Museum, Pa, USA
Shelburne Museum, Shelburne, Vermont, USA

Toys and Banks

Bethnal Green Museum, Cambridge Heath Road, London, England
Hamilton House Toy Museum, 27 Church Street, Ashbourne, Derbyshire, England
Pollock's Toy Museum, Iscala Street, London W1, England
The Toy Museum, The Grange, Rottingdean, Brighton, England
Shelburne Museum, Shelburne, Vermont, USA

General Cast Iron Items

Abbey House Museum, Kirkstall, Leeds, Yorkshire, England
Coalbrookdale Museum and Furnace Site, Telford, Shropshire, England
Mississquoi Museum, Stanbridge East, Quebec, Canada
North of England Open Air Museum, Beamish, County Durham, England. This museum displays those items found by the author at the Gulbenkian Museum of Oriental Art, Durham. It also has a collection of about 1,000 photographs of old cast iron.
Ryedale Folk Museum, Hutton-le-Hole, North Yorkshire, England
Stockport Museum, Stockport, Cheshire, England
Welsh Folk Museum, St Fagans, South Glamorgan, Wales
York Castle Museum, York, England

Bibliography

Books

Anon, *History of the Carron Company,* Bicentenary Commemorative Volume (Carron Co, 1959)

Bird, Q., *Paxton's Palace* (Cassell)

Bolton, A. T., *The Architecture of Robert and James Adam* (Country Life, 1922)

Campbell, R. H., *Carron Company* (Oliver & Boyd, 1961)

Chesters, J. N., *Iron and Steel* (World at Work Series) (London, 1948)

De Hann, D., *Household Gadgets and Appliances* (Blandford, 1930)

Farrugia, J. Y., *The Letter Box* (Centaur Press)

Gale, W. K. V., *Iron and Steel* (Moorland, 1977)

Gloag, J., *Victorian Comfort, a Social History of Design* (David and Charles, 1973)

Gloag, J. and Bridgwater, D., *A History of Cast Iron in Architecture* (Allen and Unwin, 1948)

Harris, J., *English Decorative Ironwork from Contemporary Source Books, 1693-1836* (London, Tiranti, 1960)

Herz, Louis H., *The Handbook of Old American Toys* (Mark Haber & Co, USA)

Hillier, Mary, *Automata and Mechanical Toys* (Jupiter)

Jewell, B., *Smoothing Irons* (Midas, 1978)

Long, F. J., *The Production of Iron and Steel* (Macmillan)

Marshall, J. D. and Davies-Shiel, M., *The Lake District at Work* (David and Charles, 1971)

Lindsay, J. S., *Iron and Brass Implements of the English House* (1927; London, Tiranti, 1970)

Lister, R., *Decorative Cast Ironwork in Great Britain* (Bell, 1960)

Meyer, John D. and Freeman, Larry, *Old Penny Banks* (Century House, USA)

Mitchell, James R., *Antique Metalware* (Mainstreet/Universe, USA, nd, c1977)

Norwack, M., *Kitchen Antiques* (Praeger, USA, 1975)

Owen, D., *Antique Cast Iron* (Blandford, 1977)

Raistrick, A., *Dynasty of Iron Founders – The Darbys of Coalbrookdale* (Longman, 1953; David and Charles, 1970)

Robertson, E. G., and J., *Cast Iron Decoration. A World Survey* (Thames and Hudson, 1977)

Roper, F. D., *Iron Moulding for Apprentices* (Benn)

Rothery, G. C., *Chimney Pieces and Inglenooks* (Werner Lawrie)

Schiffer, H., P., and N., *Antique Iron* (Schiffer/Moorland, 1979)

Scrivenor, Harry, *History of the Iron Trade from the Earliest Records to the Present Period* (Longman Green and Longmans)

Tripp, B. H., *The Grand Alliance: A Chapter of Industrial History* (Chantry)

Vialls, C., *Cast Iron* (A. & C. Black)

Wright, L., *Home Fires Burning* (Routledge and Keegan Paul)

Magazine Articles

Anderson, A., and Thomas, W., 'Apple Corers', *Spinning Wheel*, December 1971)

Asbee, F., 'Balconnettes — A forgotten aspect of Cast Iron', *The Connoiseur*, March 1972

Aslin, E., 'The Iron Age of Furniture', *Country Life*, 17 October 1963

Bangs, C., 'Iron Stands', *Antique Collecting*, July 1976

Bangs, C., 'Sad Irons', *Antique Collecting*, February 1976

Bland, Ann S., 'Automotive Cast Iron Toys', *Spinning Wheel*, April 1979

Breininger, L., 'Where Have All the Stove Plates Gone?' *Spinning Wheel*, December 1971

Glissman, A. H., 'A Sampling of Sad Irons', *Spinning Wheel*, July/ August 1966

Hughes, G. B., 'When Nelson and Wesley held the Door', *Country Life*, 14 March 1963

Kauffman, Henry J., 'The Charm of Cast Iron', *Spinning Wheel*, November 1970

Kelsall, G., 'Money Boxes', *Antique Collector*, June 1977

Latham, J., 'Cast Iron Door Porters in Variety', *Antique Dealer and Collectors' Guide*, September 1966

Lennox, H., 'Antique Kitchenware', *Antique Collector*, Dec 1975

Paley, W., 'Trivets from A to Z', *Spinning Wheel*, March 1971

Paley, W., 'Unusual Features in Gadget Trivets', *Spinning Wheel*, June 1977

Slemens, W., 'Liverpool's Cast Iron Churches', *Foundry Trade Journal*, 6 March 1975

Stephenson, D., 'Balcony Railings in Kent', *Archaelogia Cantaniana*, 1971

Catalogues

A selection of iron founders' catalogues consulted by the author.

Archibald Kenrick and Sons Ltd, West Bromwich, England. Established 1791. Catalogues dated 1836, 1880 and 1926.

Baldwin, Son and Company, Stourport, England. Catalogue of holloware and other kitchen equipment, door knockers, odd work, hat and coat stands, umbrella stands, boot scrapers, door porters, etc., c1898.

Carron Company, Carron, Stirlingshire, Scotland. Incorporated by Royal Charter 1759. First volume of a new catalogue of their Light Foundry Department in four sections dealing with goods relating to warming, heating and cooking, c1900.

Coalbrookdale Company, Coalbrookdale, Shropshire, England. Catalogue dated 1875.

Falkirk Ironworks, Falkirk, Scotland. Catalogue of their products, the date of which is uncertain.

Glenfield and Kennedy Ltd, Iron Founders and Hydraulic and Sanitary Engineers, Kilmarnock, Scotland. Illustrated, Descriptive and Priced Catalogue (abridged) of Waterworks Appliances. Eighth Edition, January 1914.

John Harper and Company, Ltd, Albion Works, Willenhall, Staffordshire, England. Catalogue of kitchen equipment, builders' and general hardware, c1932.

Samuel Gratrix Jr and Brother, Alport Works, Quay Street, Deansgate, Manchester, England. Illustrated catalogue of Sanitary Appliances. No 167, c1910.

Smith and Wellstood Ltd, Columbian Stove Works, Bonnybridge, Scotland. Illustrated catalogue No 5/04 and price list of patented and registered American portable cooking stoves, kitchen ranges, warming stoves, ship's galley ranges, cabin stoves, portable boilers etc, c1904.

Walter Macfarlane and Company, Saracen Foundry, Washington Street and Possil Park, Glasgow, Scotland. Fifth edition of their catalogue of castings. Published 1870/1

William Cross and Son Ltd, Lyng Foundry, West Bromwich, Staffordshire, England. Established 1835. Catalogue of general ironwork No 34, c1934.

Acknowledgements

Without the help of a large number of individuals who were kind enough to allow access to their collections of cast iron it would have been impossible to accumulate my library of about 1,500 photographs of 'Collectable Cast Iron' and their aid is most gratefully acknowledged. In addition, the following cheerfully gave assistance to an exceptional degree and to them I owe a considerable debt of gratitude:

Mr H. L. Ames, Bedford, Quebec, Canada, who discovered much of interest in the Eastern United States and Canada. Mr W. Jackson, Cockermouth, Cumbria, for the loan of old catalogues. Mr Hugh Kenrick and members of Archibald Kenrick and Sons Ltd, for the loan of old catalogues. The staff of all the museums visited. The staff of the libraries at Wilmslow, Cheshire and in particular at Cockermouth, Cumbria, whose efforts to obtain books of reference were tireless.

Acknowledgement is gratefully given to the following for the use of illustrations: H. L. Ames, 200, 213-5; Brian Jewell/Broadwater Collection Library, 29; Archibald Kenrick & Sons Ltd, 164; N. Madan, Darjeeling, 55; N. Milner, 17, 18; The Post Office, 253-4. All the remaining photographs were taken by the author.

The following have kindly given permission to photograph cast iron items in their possession: Abbey House Museum, Leeds, 185, 227-9; M. Barrowclough, 167, 175, 180; Beck Isle Museum, Pickering, Yorkshire, 358; Bewdley Museum, Worcestershire, 360; Mrs Blair, Berwick on Tweed, 76, 236, 309, 361; O. Blair, Bedford, Quebec, 353; Bolling Hall Museum, Bradford, 46-7, 177-8, 190, 220-3, 226, 348; M. Bracegirdle, Macclesfield, 224; Bowes Museum, Barnard Castle, Co Durham, 35; Mrs H. W. Capel, Sherbrooke, Quebec, 301, 311, 354; Castle Museum, York, 161, 166, 188, 230, 241-2; Mrs Corey, Bedford, Quebec, 63, 205, 216, 342; R. T. Cowern, Whitehaven, 138; P. Farmer, Allanton by Duns, 160, 171, 174, 179, 181, 352; Mrs W. Fisher, Pickering Yorkshire, 151, 157; W. Forsythe, 239; Gloucester City Museum (Bishop Hooper's Lodgings), 30, 34, 105-7, 110, 355; J. A. Hope, Lorton, 256-8; Ironbridge Gorge Museum Trust, 31, 248-9, 259; Mr Kelley, Macclesfield, 158, 221, 225, 308, 335, 344-5; N. Kennon, Cockermouth, 140, 159, 193, 195, 260, 373; Archibald Kenrick & Sons Ltd, 183, 191, 374; Mr Litt, Cockermouth, 331; Mississquoi Museum, Quebec, 62, 111-12, 200, 204, 215, 265, 297-9, 302-3, 305, 334, 337-8, 356; T. Morgan, Seascale, Cumbria, 347; Museum of Lakeland Life and Industry, Kendal, 82, 98, 101; Newport Museum and Art Gallery, Monmouthshire, 73, 170, 233, 243-5; North of England Open Air Museum, Beamish, County Durham (originally at the Gulbenkian Museum of Oriental Art, University of Durham), 168, 173, 182, 186, 231, 234, 237-8;

Rev R. Pitches, Lorton, Cumbria, 162, 336; Miss Pope and Miss Motz, Rock Forest, Quebec, 53, 56, 65, 104, 122-137, 213-14, 367-8; L. Rennie, Athelstan, Quebec, 23, 66-7; Mrs Rogers, Beadnall, Northumberland, 44, 74-5, 176; Rufford Old Hall, Ormskirk (National Trust), 41; Rushland Hall, Newby Bridge, 154, 359; Miss D. Ryall, 209; Rydale Folk Museum, Hutton-le-Hole, Yorkshire, 32-3, 52, 54; Sizergh Castle, Kendal (National Trust), 36, 350; Shelburne Museum, Vermont, 57-61, 64, 68-9, 94, 109, 124, 199, 201-3, 206-8, 263-4, 266-296, 300, 304, 306, 312-26, 332, 346, 351, 366, 369-71, 377, 379; Stockport Museum, 218, 221, 333; J. Tyson, Lorton, Cumbria, 357; Wallington House (National Trust), 38, 40, 42, 92, 211-12; E. Walker, Eyam, Derbyshire, 189, 232, 246; Welsh Folk Museum, St Fagans, 165, 169, 172, 192, 364-5; Wetheriggs Pottery, Penrith, 99, 251; Whitehaven Museum, 255, 339-40.

Index

air bricks, 8
Adam, R. & J., 15
altar piece, 115, 124
apple peelers and corers, 72, 80-1
arcades, 8
ash guards, 25, 28, 35, 133

balconies, 13, 16
balusters, 8
balustrades, 16
bandstands, 8, 18
banks, 9, 102, 105, 108, 114-19
bannerettes, 15, 18
baths, 41-2, 45
'Bath' grates, 29
bells, 15
bell pulls, 60-1, 65
benches, 100-1
Berlin Black, 37, 132
bollards, 9
boot jacks, 115, 123, 134
boot scrapers, 8, 60-1, 65-6
braziers, 15
buildings:
    Chatsworth House, 9
    Coal Exchange, 21
    Corio Villa, 21
    Crystal Palace, 8, 9
    Durbar Hall, 21
    Haughwout, 21
    Norfolk Customs House, 13
    Palace of Westminster (Houses
        of Parliament),9
    Royal Scottish Museum, 8
    Smithfield Meat Market, 21
    St George's, Liverpool, 8
    St Michael's, Liverpool, 8
    St Paul's Cathedral, 15
buttons, 9

candlesticks, 9, 22
cannon, 7, 10, 115
'Carronade', 10, 11
chairs, 100
cheese press, 125

clothes washer, 46
churches, 8, 18
church pulpits, 9
cinder sifters, 9, 36
cleaning, 132-3
cloches, 9
clock case, 122
coat, hat & umbrella stands, 8,
    10, 61, 70
coffee mills, 8, 72, 79
coffee pots, 79
coffee roaster, 80
columns, 8, 15-16, 20
cork screw, 128
cork squeezer, 96, 120
crosses, 15, 18
curb, see fender

dog grates, 25, 27, 35
door furniture:
    handles, 65
    knobs, 8, 60-1
    knockers, 8, 60-4, 131
    latches, 8
    letter slots, 60-2
door porters, 8, 61-5, 71-8, 132
Dutch ovens, 12

electro bronze, 37, 132
Ezard, C., 28, 131, 133

fenders, 25-6, 28, 35
finials, 8, 15-16
fire backs, 7, 11-12, 23-6
fire dogs, 7
fire grate, see also miniature grates
    10, 26-7, 31
fire irons, 26
fire iron rests, 36-7
flag poles, 8, 15, 18
fountains, 13
    drinking, 8, 41-4
Franklin, Benjamin, 27, 30
Franklin stoves, 30
fruit slicers, 72, 82

gas cookers, 8, 37
    fires, 39
    rings, 39
    stoves, 39
gates, 13, 16, 18, 20, 21
goffering (gauffering) irons, see
    irons
gold changer, 126
grates, 8, 16
grave slabs, 7
griddle, 83
gutters, 18

hat & coat pins, 8, 96, 120
hinges, 8, 11
hitching post, 129
    weight, 129
hob grates, 25, 27, 29, 31, 35
holloware, 8
horseshoes, 11
houses, 18

Iron Bridge, 8
iron making and casting, 7-9
irons:
    ball, 49, 51, 55
    billiard table, 43
    box, 8, 43, 47-8, 51
    charcoal, 43, 48, 50-1
    crimping, 50, 52
    egg, 49, 55
    electric, 43, 49, 51
    fluting, 46, 55
    gas, 43, 49, 51-4
    goffering, 49
    heater, 43, 47-9
    Italian ('tally'), 8, 49-51, 55
    laundry, 36, 46
    mushroom, 49, 51
    petrol, 51
    piping, 51, 55
    Potts, 43, 48, 50-1
    puffing, 55
    sad, 8, 12, 42, 46-7, 50
    sleeve, 55

spirit, 43, 50-1
tailor's ('goose'), 42, 49, 53-4
iron stands, 49, 56-9

Japanned Black, 37, 132

kettles, 9, 12, 70, 80
kitchen range, 26, 31
knife cleaners, 72, 82

'lace work', 19, 21
lamps, 9, 12, 16, 18-19, 22, 98
laundry stoves, 36, 46
lavatory stands, 45
letter box, 98-9, 101

maize grinders & shellers, 72, 78
mangles, 46
manhole covers, 9
marmalade slicers, 72, 82
match safe, 115, 121, 123
mileposts, 9
miniature grates, 84-8
mirror, picture & photo frames,
    45, 125
mortar & pestle, 83
'morte safe', 9
muffin dish, 83

nails, 8-9, 11
nameplates, 9, 98-9
Nash, John, 15
notices, 9

ornaments, 9, 89-94, 128
ovens, 30-1

pans, 9, 11-12, 26, 70
pagodas, 15
painting, 132-3
paper weights, 121
plaques, 9, 95-8
post protectors, 129
potato masher, 81
pots, 7, 9, 10-12, 26, 28, 69-70,
    78-9
public conveniences, 9, 41-2
pumps, 40-1

railings, 8, 13, 15-18, 20, 61
railway stations, 18
registration marks, 131
Rumford, Count, 27, 29

scales, 72, 81
seal presses, 115, 122

seats, 9, 13
sewing machines, 127
shovels, 9, 36
sign posts, 9
snow roller, 126
spittoons, 8, 112, 120
stairs, 18
stands (toast, kettle, hearth), 36, 38
stationers' sundries, 112, 120
statues, 13
Stevens, A., 115, 124
stoves, 12, 26-37
string dispensers, 121
sugar nippers, 120
sundials, 9

tables, 9, 46, 101-2, 122
tea pots, 9
telephone kiosks, 98, 101
terminals, 15, 18, 19
'tidy Betty', see ash guard
toaster, 83
tobacco cutters, 120
    jars, 115, 124
    pipes, 9
tools, 11
toys, 9, 102-13
trade tokens, 9
trivets, 8, 35-6, 38-9, 56-9

umbrella stands, 8, 10, 61, 67-9
urns, 115, 124, 127-8

vases, 13
ventilators, 20

waffle irons, 83
weather vanes, 15, 18
weights, 8
windows, 8, 13, 22

Iron founders, Britain
Allied Ironfounders, 9-10
Baldwin, Son & Co, 9, 63, 78-9,
    112
Bowling Ironworks, 63
Branthwaite, J., 46
Brede Furnace, 23
Carron Co, 10-11, 13, 29, 30, 37-8,
    53, 70, 132
Coalbrookdale Co, 7-10, 13, 17-18,
    60, 62-3, 65, 67, 73, 100
Cockran & Co, 99
Cross, William & Son, 8, 36, 38-9,
    43, 47-9, 53, 56
Crowley & Co, 89, 115, 124

Dale Co, see Coalbrookdale Co
Darby, Abraham, see Coalbrook-
    dale Co

Falkirk Ironworks, 10, 60, 62-3, 65,
    75
Glenfield & Kennedy, 43
Gratrix, S., 45
Harper, J., 38, 54, 62, 82, 114
Hillary, J., 46
James, W., 71
Jones, T.J., 62
Kenrick, Archibald, & Sons, 8, 10,
    14, 38, 48, 51, 55, 60-6, 71, 76,
    78, 131-2
Macfarlane, Walter, & Co, 8,
    10-11, 14, 17-19, 21, 40-1, 43, 98
Pallisher, 46
Rowbotham, R., 92
Salter, 47
Sheldon, T., & Co, 47
Smith & Hawkes, 99
Smith & Wellstood, 14, 29, 31, 83
Yates, R., 30

Iron founders, America
Architectural Ironworks, 18
Bartlett, Robbins & Co, see
    Hayward, Bartlett & Co
Beckwith, P.D., 35
Carlisle Ironworks, 12
Carpenter, 112
Chase Bros, 13
Colebrookdale Iron Co, 57
Elizabeth Furnace, 12
Enterprise Manufacturing Co, 57,
    79
Finely, C.F., 32, 36
Goddel Co, 80
Granger Bros, 32
Hall, J., 102, 114
Hayward, Bartlett & Co, 13, 18
Hill, N.N., Brass Co, 106
Hinderer's Ironworks, 13, 18
Hubley, 108, 112
Ives, E.R., 112
Jenks, J., 11
Leeds Ironworks, 13
Lorio Ironworks, 13
Marlbro Furnace, 12
McCann, J., 129
Mott, J.L., 13
New York Wire Railing Co, 18
Potts, S. & J., 12
Saugus Ironworks, 11, 26
Shakespeare Ironworks, 13

Stevens, J & E., 108, 112, 116, 118, 119
Stevens, L., 12
Stiegel, H. W., 12
Swan Co, 49
Tyson Furnace, 34
Weedon, 112
Wood, R., 13
Zane, I., 12

Iron founders, Canada
Horskin, H., 33
Ives, H. R., 58
Kerr & Coombes, 57
McClary, 34
Moffat Stove Co, 36